MEDITATIONS
⤳ FROM
WORLD RELIGIONS

MEDITATIONS FROM WORLD RELIGIONS

Originally published as
QUIET STRENGTH FROM WORLD RELIGIONS

Copyright © 1960 by Quinter Marcellus Lyon

Library of Congress catalog card number: 60-7957

For permission to quote copyrighted material, grateful acknowledgment is made to the authors, publishers, and copyright owners of books listed below and in the additional Acknowledgments and Bibliography Sources (pp. 229-232).

The John Day Company: *Confucius: the Man and the Myth* by H. G. Creel, copyright 1949 by H. G. Creel.

Harper & Brothers: *Bhagavad-Gita: The Song of God* by Swami Prabhavananda and Christopher Isherwood, copyright 1944 by Vedanta Society of Southern California.

The Macmillan Company: *The World's Greatest Scriptures* by Lewis Browne, copyright 1946 by Lewis Browne. *A Short History of Chinese Philosophy* by Fung Yu-lan, ed. by Derk Bodde, copyright 1948 by The Macmillan Company.

The Macmillan Company (and George Allen & Unwin, Ltd.): *Religion and Society* by S. Radhakrishnan, copyright 1947 by The Macmillan Company. *The Analects of Confucius* by Arthur Waley, copyright 1938 by The Macmillan Company. *Three Ways of Thought in Ancient China* by Arthur Waley, copyright 1939 by The Macmillan Company.

Thomas Nelson and Sons: *The Apocrypha*, Revised Standard Version, copyright 1957 by the Division of Christian Education of the National Council of Churches. All Biblical quotations are from The Revised Standard Version of the Bible, copyright 1946 and 1952 by the Division of Christian Education of the National Council of Churches of Christ in the U. S. A.

Printed in U.S.A.

MEDITATIONS FROM WORLD RELIGIONS

QUINTER M. LYON

New York   ABINGDON PRESS   Nashville

To
Donna Lyon Keck
and
David Beekley Lyon

CONTENTS

PREFACE

At no time in the history of man has there been such need as now for a book of meditations in the great religions. Such a book should accomplish two things. First, it will help to make religion vital by promoting the systematic cultivation of religious attitudes and insights. Second, it will free us from religious provincialism in this age of intercontinental ballistic missiles. As our world grows smaller each day, there is an increasing need to understand and appreciate the values in cultures other than our own.

These meditations are not intended as an effort toward religious syncretism. Each scripture is offered for its sheer value, with no subtle implications beyond its intrinsic worth. Our first duty is to understand our own traditions and to be faithful to the best in them. But too many stop there, not realizing that other traditions have produced great prophets and that it is our privilege to make their intimate acquaintance. "Bow down and worship where others kneel," said Ramakrishna, "for where so many have been paying tribute of adoration the kind Lord must manifest himself, for he is all mercy." The name by which God is called is not so important as one's devotion to God's truth and love.

Without dogmatism I offer these meditations, each based upon a selected passage of scripture. In making the selections it has been my policy to use only the best. The scripture is followed by an explanation or commentary. Finally, there is a moment of dedication to whatever is universal in the passage.

These pages are intended as a small contribution to universal understanding and good will.

January, 1960   Q.M.L.

MEDITATIONS FROM WORLD RELIGIONS

1 LET THERE BE LIGHT

In the beginning God created the heavens and the earth. The earth was without form and void, and darkness was upon the face of the deep; and the Spirit of God was moving over the face of the waters.

And God said, "Let there be light"; and there was light. And God saw that the light was good. . . .

And God said, "Let the earth bring forth living creatures according to their kinds: cattle and creeping things and beasts of the earth according to their kinds." And it was so. And God made the beasts of the earth according to their kinds and the cattle according to their kinds, and everything that creeps upon the ground according to its kind. And God saw that it was good.

GENESIS 1:1-4, 24-25

If this were to be taken as a literal, scientific account of creation, it would have little value. But as an expression of the mystery of creation and of our total dependence upon God, it is most significant. From God we come, to God we return. "In him we live and move and have our being." So also with nature as a whole. It is a mystery which gives us joy in contemplation. Even God "saw that it was good." Certainly we cannot get the most out of life without the faith that "this is my Father's world" and that it is good to be alive.

Have science and civilization removed us too far from the primeval sense of grateful dependence upon nature and nature's God?

GOD GIVE US JOY in the mere act of living. May his light shine in our hearts. Amen.

1

O Ahura Mazda, this I ask of thee: speak to me truly!
Who was the first father of Justice by giving birth to him?
Who established the sunlit days and the star glistering sphere and
   the Milky Way?
Who, apart from thee, established the law by which the moon
   waxes and wanes?
These and other things would I like to know!

O Ahura Mazda, this I ask of thee: speak to me truly!
Who was from beneath sustaining the earth and the clouds
So that they would not fall down? Who made the waters and the
   plants?
Who yoked the two swift ones, thunder and lightning, to the
   wind and to the clouds?
Who is the creator of Good Disposition?

O Ahura Mazda, this I ask of thee: speak to me truly!
Who produced well-made lights and darkness?
Who produced sleep, well-induced through laborious waking?
Who produced the dawns and the noon through the contrast with
   the night
Whose daily changes act for the enlightened believers as monitors
   of their interests? . . .

O Ahura Mazda, this I ask of thee: speak to me truly!
Who shaped prized Love with Power?
Who, by guidance, rendered sons reverent to their fathers?
It is I who strive to learn to recognize thee
Through the bounteous Mentality, as giver of all good things!

YASNA 44.3-5, 7

These words of the Persian prophet Zoroaster are believed to have been written perhaps a century before the

creation story of Genesis 1. Both writers conceived of God as great and as one. Zoroaster was the more lyric. We need the poetic mind in order to appreciate the truth of creation. Scientific accounts of origins leave the essential mysteries unsolved. How amazing that everything dovetails in the universe—sun and moon, stars and planets, light and darkness, clouds and winds, night and morning, sleep and waking, labor and rest, life and gratitude, parents and children, government and good citizenship. With all our disorder, there is yet a fundamental order in all things. The Persians recognized it, as did the Jews. It is a clue to God's being.

The modern age may need to be reminded that even the pattern of the world constitutes a matchless mystery.

O GOD, how marvelous are the secrets of thy universe and of thy creature man! How great thou art, O God. Amen.

3 LIFE'S GOODNESS

ANCIENT EGYPT

(To Aton—the sun:)
Bright is the earth when thou risest in the horizon;
When thou shinest as Aton by day
Thou drivest away the darkness.
When thou sendest forth thy rays,
The Two Lands (Egypt) are in daily festivity.
Men waken and stand upon their feet
When thou hast raised them up.
Their limbs bathed, they take their clothing,
Their arms uplifted in adoration to thy dawning.
Then in all the world they do their work.

This is part of the famous "Hymn to the Sun" by the Egyptian Pharaoh Amenhotep IV, who renamed himself

Ikhnaton in honor of Aton, the divine sun. Here was a kind of monotheism more than a century before Moses is believed to have given the law to Israel. Of all the elements of nature, the sun was chosen as the most representative force on which human life and all other life depends. In the hymn Ikhnaton is really expressing gratitude to God for the joy of living.

Despite our disappointment with the world at times, our reluctance to leave it would seem to indicate that we think it is good.

O God, may we find thee in the common experiences of nature: in the warmth of the sun, the refreshment of the rain, the light of the working day, the darkness of restful night; and in the cycle of birth and death, hunger and satisfaction. Amen.

4 NATURE'S LAWS

HINDUISM

. . . The far-refulgent mornings make apparent the lovely treasures which the darkness covered.
The one departeth and the other cometh; unlike in hue day's halves march on successive.
One hides the gloom of the surrounding parents. Dawn on the shining chariot is resplendent.
The same in form today, the same tomorrow, they still keep Varuna's eternal statute. . . .   RIG-VEDA 1.123.6-8

This Vedic poem from ancient India may have been in existence more than three thousand years ago. It reveals an attitude of aesthetic reverence for nature's beneficence and regularity. The Indo-Aryans believed Varuna to be a sky-god who was responsible for the wonders of the world. In worshiping him they were really expressing their appreciation of universal beauty and their gratitude for the gifts of God. Their perception of the regularity of nature foreshadowed the concept of natural law, suggesting a maturing insight into God's being and his oneness.

Is a religion of nature sufficient for our spiritual needs? Psalm 19 would seem incomplete without its reverence for God's spiritual gifts.

O GOD, reveal thyself to us in the sublimity of universal law, as in the beauty of the snowflake, that we may adore thee. Amen.

5 NATURE AND SPIRIT

HINDUISM

(To Varuna—a sky god:)
None, verily, hath ever let or hindered this the most wise god's
    mighty deed of magic,
Whereby with all their flood, the lucid rivers fill not one sea
    wherein they pour their waters.

If we have sinned against the man who loves us, have ever
    wronged a brother, friend, or comrade,
The neighbor ever with us, or a stranger, O Varuna, remove from
    us the trespass.   RIG-VEDA 5.85, 6-7

Like Psalm 19, this Vedic poem includes wonder at nature's mysterious marvels and also a deep regard for the moral law. Varuna is here viewed as lord of both natural and ethical realms. As for nature, modern science "explains" that the vapor arising to form the clouds balances the water pouring into the oceans, in an endless cycle. But does our knowledge of nature remove any of its essential mystery? In the realm of spirit we note that moral obligation extends even to strangers. Divine forgiveness is needed and ready when through human weakness one sins.

When we break a natural law, nature usually heals us. Does God's beneficent spirit heal our souls when we repent of transgressing a moral law?

O GOD, speak to our conscience. May we seek thy forgiveness when we have sinned. Heal us and inspire us. Amen.

6 GOD'S NEARNESS

ISLAM

Is he not closer than the vein of thy neck? Thou needest not raise thy voice, for he knoweth the secret whisper, and what is yet more hidden. . . . He knows what is in the land and in the sea; no leaf falleth but he knoweth it; nor is there a grain in the darkness under the earth, nor a thing, green or sere, but it is recorded.   KORAN 6:12, 59

The East and the West is God's: therefore, whichever way ye turn, there is the face of God: Truly God is immense, knowing (omnipresent, omniscient).   KORAN 2:109

We have done Muhammad an injustice by picturing his God as a "man in the sky"—a kind of Oriental potentate. This passage from the Koran is comparable with Tennyson's "higher pantheism." Neither Tennyson nor Muhammad identifies God with the physical world. Both use highly figurative language. Consider Tennyson:

The sun, the moon, the stars, the seas, the hills and the
 plains—
Are not these, O Soul, the Vision of Him who reigns?

Is not the Vision He? tho' He be not that which He seems?
Dreams are true while they last, and do we not live in
 dreams?

Earth, these solid stars, this weight of body and limb,
Are they not sign and symbol of thy division from Him?

Dark is the world to thee: thyself art the reason why;
For is He not all but thou, that hast power to feel "I am I?"

Glory about thee, without thee; and thou fulfillest thy
 doom,
Making Him broken gleams, and a stifled splendor and
 gloom.

Speak to Him thou for He hears, and Spirit with Spirit can
 meet—
Closer is He than breathing, and nearer than hands and
 · feet.

God is law, say the wise; O Soul, and let us rejoice,
For if He thunder by law the thunder is yet His voice.

Our only fear should be that we estrange ourselves from
God's being by failing to share in his goodness.

O GOD ABOVE US, beneath us, within us, satisfy our hearts
with the joy of thy presence. Amen.

7 YEARNING FOR GOD

As a hart longs
for flowing streams,
so longs my soul
for thee, O God.
My soul thirsts for God,
for the living God.
When shall I come and behold
the face of God?
My tears have been my food
day and night,
while men say to me continually,
"Where is your God?"

PSALM 42:1-3

Man needs God as the body needs water. It is as St. Augustine said:

Thou didst make us for thyself, and restless
are our hearts till they find rest in thee.

Yet in our search for God we often feel frustrated. Those are the times when anxiety rides hard upon us, and we cannot seem to get through to God, who would quiet our fears. Men seeing us in trouble taunt us with the reproach, "Where is your God?" In such seasons faith is doubly needful. Souls thus tried need God most. His filling of our need is not mechanical, like turning on the water faucet. Some people find God gradually, perceiving him first perhaps in the beauty of nature or the power of the storm, then in human relations, and finally in the depths of their own souls.

8

Can such a persistent need as ours for God be illusory?

> Why are you cast down, O my soul,
>   and why are you disquieted within me?
> Hope in God; for I shall again praise him,
>   my help and my God. Amen.

PSALM 42:11

8   EARLY SEEK HIM

OLD TESTAMENT

Seek the Lord while he may be found,
  call upon him while he is near;
let the wicked forsake his way,
  and the unrighteous man his thoughts;
let him return to the Lord, that he may have mercy on him,
  and to our God, for he will abundantly pardon.
For my thoughts are not your thoughts,
  neither are your ways my ways, says the Lord.
For as the heavens are higher than the earth,
  so are my ways higher than your ways,
  and my thoughts than your thoughts.

ISAIAH 55:6-9

"Early" means "today." For anything that needs to be done, there is never any better time than now. This is true in the case of the search for God. To feel unworthy of such a lofty enterprise is no good reason for denying ourselves the joy of God's companionship, for God is merciful. He desires not our punishment but our salvation. He does not deal with us as a proud ruler might deal with a subject. "My ways are higher than your ways, and my thoughts than your thoughts" means that God does not react to us in the ways that a man would react. God's truth is objective, and his desire is for the fulfillment of the human spirit.

That he is so much higher than we are means, in part, that he is infinite in his perfection, his might, and his redemptive love.

O GOD, with humble reverence for thy great power, may we still know thee as a friend. Amen.

9 THE FRIENDLY UNIVERSE

HINDUISM

> (*To Agni—the divine Fire:*)
> *To thee, dispeller of the night, O Agni, day by day with prayer*
> *Bringing thee reverence, we come*
> *Ruler of sacrifices, guard of Law eternal, radiant One,*
> *Increasing in thine own abode.*
> *Be to us easy of approach, even as a father to his son.*
>
> RIG-VEDA 1.1

This hymn is addressed to Agni, the god of fire or the divine fire itself. It reveals primitive man's reverence for the beneficent powers of nature; it expresses his desire to be on intimate terms with the deity. Agni is likened to a father. God's ways are not so much "higher than your ways" that he cannot be readily approached. Neither nature nor God desires that man should feel separated from nature's bounty and God's love.

We need to think of God and nature as friendly, fatherly, or motherly. Our modern ideas of God may become so naturalistic or sophisticated that he is no longer "easy of approach, even as a father to his son."

O GOD, may we recognize thee in the beneficence and awesomeness of the fire, the storm, and the harvest; but most of all in the strength and affection of fatherhood, and in thine own abode of spiritual excellence. Amen.

10 KNOWING THE TRUE GOD

HINDUISM

Agni, Vayu, Aditya, Kala . . . Rudra, Vishnu . . . These are but the chief manifestations of the highest, the immortal, the incorporeal Brahman. . . . Brahman, indeed, is all this, and a man may meditate on, worship or discard also those which are its manifestations.   MAITRI UPANISHAD 4.5-6

This passage from the Maitri Upanishad has great significance in the Hindu tradition. In a land of polytheism and idolatry many thoughtful hearts perceived that there was really only one God, though he was known by different names. The different names suggested various qualities of the one spiritual ("incorporeal") God, as Agni suggested his burning quality and Vishnu his sustaining power. The thoughtful philosopher-prophets called the true God Brahman—which merely means the one true, living, absolutely real God.

Are we repelled by a strange religion on account of its name for God? We need to realize God as an experience, not as a name.

O GOD, by whatever name we call thee, may we adore thee and find thy motivating presence to be satisfying. Amen.

Verily, in the beginning this world was Brahman, the limitless one—limitless to the east, limitless to the north . . . limitless in every direction. . . . Incomprehensible is that supreme Soul, unlimited, unborn, not to be reasoned about, unthinkable—he whose soul is space! In the dissolution of the world he alone remains awake. From that space, he, assuredly, awakes this world, which is a mass of thought. It is thought by him, and in him it disappears. His is that shining form which gives heat in yonder sun and which is the brilliant light in a smokeless fire, as also the fire in the stomach which cooks the food. For thus it has been said: "He who is in the fire, and he who is here in the heart, and he who is yonder in the sun—he is one." MAITRI UPANISHAD 6.17

In this passage from the Maitri Upanishad we may perceive a universal truth. Hinduism is often condemned lightly because it is said to be pantheistic. But in these noble lines Brahman is not identified with nature. Brahman remains everlastingly real even when the worlds are dissolved. Nor is reality materialistic, but rather ideal—"a mass of thought." Finally, God is recognized as "in the heart." And God in the heart is one with nature's God.

Can finite man know an infinite God? By exploiting his own creativity and his capacity for love and goodness, it seems that man may enter into the very heart of God.

O THOU ETERNAL BEING "whose robe is the universe" but whose majesty can be harbored in the human heart, take from our souls all pettiness and move us to greatness. Amen.

12

"Bring hither a fig from there."
"Here it is, Sir."
"Divide it."
"It is divided, Sir."
"What do you see there?"
"These rather fine seeds, Sir."
"Of these, please, divide one."
"It is divided, Sir."
"What do you see there?"
"Nothing at all, Sir."
Then he said to him: "Verily, my dear, that finest essence which you do not perceive—verily, my dear, from that finest essence this great Nyagrodha tree thus arises. Believe me, my dear," said he, "that which is the finest essence—this whole world has that as its self. That is Reality. That is Atman. That art thou, Svetaketu. . . ." CHANDOGYA UPANISHAD 6.12.1-3

No greater philosophic reverence has ever been expressed than this insight into the invisible power at the heart of things. In this passage from the Chandogya Upanishad, Svetaketu's teacher assures him that his own spiritual personality is intimately akin to God, that he is a child of God, made in his very image. In a profound sense, he and God are one. Nature's God is personal—the Atman, or Absolute Self.

It is not irreverent to think of ourselves as being essentially one with God. The idea is found in the New Testament also. See John 14:20; 15:5; 17:21; Acts 17:28.

O GOD, create in us the true image of thyself in wisdom, goodness, and selfless love, that we may commune with thee in our inmost heart. Amen.

13   UNION WITH GOD

Turiya is not that which is conscious of the inner world, nor that which is conscious of the outer world, nor that which is conscious of both, nor that which is a mass of consciousness. It is not simple consciousness nor is it unconsciousness. It is unperceived, unrelated, incomprehensible, uninferable, unthinkable, and indescribable. The essence of the Consciousness manifesting as the self, it is the cessation of all phenomena; it is all peace, all bliss, and non-dual.   MANDUKYA UPANISHAD 7

Turiya—meaning "fourth"—refers to that kind of consciousness which is neither waking nor dreaming, a consciousness even deeper than that of dreamless sleep. Here in the Mandukya Upanishad the mystic is trying to describe what by his own admission is indescribable. He tries to tell what God is by saying what he is not. God cannot be perceived physically. Nor can he be related, for that would make him dependent on that to which he is related. He cannot be comprehended, for that would make him smaller than that which comprehends him. To be inferred by logic would reduce him to something less than absolute truth. The sure conclusion is that God is absolute unity, all bliss, and all peace. Such is the beatific vision.

Who does not want to be happy—supremely happy? What could possibly make us happier than the knowledge of God's presence?

O GOD, remove from our hearts the clutter of haste, anger, fear, and envy, that we may have room for the abundance of thy spirit. Amen.

14

As, from a blazing fire, sparks essentially akin to it fly forth by the thousand, so also, my good friend, do various beings come forth from the imperishable Brahman and unto Him again return.
MUNDAKA UPANISHAD 2.1.1

In the figure of the fire and the sparks we are reminded of the fleeting nature of the sparks in contrast with the continuing fire. So the Psalmist compares man with the grass of the field, and the Preacher reminds us that the soul goes back to God, from whence it came. Josiah Royce, the great American philosopher—like Ramanuja, the Hindu philosopher—tries to show how the individual soul, being of the essence of God, can be completely dependent on him and yet retain its essential individuality, as it lives on eternally in God.

If we share God's being, how can we ever sin? On the other hand, how can we have personal integrity if we live wholly within God, who molds our lives? If we are the breath of God's spirit, should we not try to understand ourselves and the God whose being we mysteriously share?

O GOD, give us the patience to persist in philosophical reflection on the nature of life and our relationship to thee. Help us not to despise our human nature, for we have come forth from thee and seek ever to realize our kinship with thee. Amen.

*Thou art woman, thou art man; thou art youth, thou art
maiden; thou, as an old man, totterest along on thy staff; thou
art born with thy face turned everywhere.*

SHVETASHVATARA UPANISHAD 4.3

This dramatic passage from a late Upanishad is obviously figurative. Taken prosaically it has little value, but with imagination we can understand that God can be discerned in the virtues and mysteries of womanhood, in the vigor and spiritual potentialities of manhood, and in the human and inanimate processes of all of nature. Said Whitehead, "God is *in* the world, or nowhere, creating continually in us and around us. This creative principle is everywhere, in animate and so-called inanimate matter, in the ether, water, earth, human hearts. . . . In so far as man partakes of this creative process does he partake of the divine, of God."

If God is the old man trembling on his staff, then God must share the suffering as well as the wisdom of old age.

O God, grant that we may see thy face in nature, thy love in motherhood, thy strength in fatherhood, thy goodness in the beauty of youth, thy compassion in all the processes of life. May we find joy in the divine vision. Amen.

God is one; there is no second. The One is everywhere.
Search in thy heart; there is His abode.
O men and women, seek the sanctuary of the One.
He pervadeth thy body and the universe as well. . . .
I have met God who dwells within the heart. . . .
The soul that is joined with him is indestructible. . . .

GRANTH

The mystical prophet-poet Kabir contributed many verses to the Sikh Bible. The scripture above is typical of his reverent monotheism. His delight is in paradox, as when he asserts that God is one, although he is not one thing at any time or place in space. He is everywhere in space, although his essence is not spatial. He pervades the body—all bodies—but he is to be found only by searching the heart. He who knows the ways of a poet will realize that Kabir means to say that God is spirit, vivifying and transforming earthly life into a heaven, inspiring inward peace and good will. Such transformation occurs only when we search and find God in that inner heart of ours.

Have we perhaps missed finding him by being too literal-minded?

O GOD, may we on looking into our hearts truly find thee and not some unlovely spirit of selfish hate. If our hearts are thy proper abode, may we keep them pure and loving. Amen.

Men of Athens, I perceive that in every way you are very religious. For as I passed along, and observed the objects of your worship, I found also an altar with this inscription, "To an unknown god." What therefore you worship as unknown, this I proclaim to you. The God who made the world and everything in it, being Lord of heaven and earth, does not live in shrines made by man, nor is he served by human hands, as though he needed anything, since he himself gives to all men life and breath and everything. And he made from one every nation of men to live on all the face of the earth, having determined allotted periods and the boundaries of their habitation, that they should seek God, in the hope that they might feel after him and find him. Yet he is not far from each one of us, for

"In him we live and move and have our being";
as even some of your poets have said,
"For we are indeed his offspring."
Being then God's offspring, we ought not to think that the Deity is like gold, or silver, or stone, a representation by the art and imagination of man. The times of ignorance God overlooked, but now he commands all men everywhere to repent. . . .

ACTS 17:22-30

There is no denying the fact that some people know God better than others do. In comparing certain primitive religious traditions with more advanced ones, it seems evident that God has been more fully discovered or revealed in the advanced than in the primitive. So also in the cases of individuals in the same tradition. One person is more attentive to the influence of the prophets than another. One has meditated more deeply concerning the nature of God and virtue than another. By the grace of God we may belong to the enlightened tradition rather than to the primitive. By his grace we may have come under the influence of men of true greatness. If so, we are indeed privileged partakers of eternity.

One thing is certain: we need to know the other traditions intimately before we can judge how truly God is known in them. Can we say that "our" God is the "known" God if we ourselves do not know him well?

O GOD, accept the gift of ourselves as we dedicate our wills to thee, whom we would know better. Amen.

18 GOD'S ULTIMATE MYSTERY

TAOISM

Something there is, whose veiled creation was
Before the earth or sky began to be;
So silent, so aloof and so alone,
It changes not, nor fails, but touches all:
Conceive it as the mother of the world. . . .

Man conforms to the earth;
The earth conforms to the sky;
The sky conforms to the Way;
The Way conforms to its own nature.

TAO TÊ CHING 25

. . . .

The Way is a void,
Used but never filled. . . .
It is like a preface to God.

TAO TÊ CHING 4

. . . .

The Way eternal has no name.

TAO TÊ CHING 32

Is there some danger that we may assume too much familiarity with God? The Taoist scriptures warn us against just that. The Tao Tê Ching insists that God is unique, ultimately comparable to nothing that we know. He is not a thing like other things, nor a man like other men, nor one cause among other causes and effects. Nor is God a simple source like other sources. Everything in the world conforms to the Way, but the Way conforms to nothing but its own nature. Said the Taoist Chuang Tzu, "No one knows where its contents come from and so it is spoken of as the 'containing light.'" By living in the Way, neither striving nor complaining, we are entering into God's being. The Way is "like a preface to God." Reverence should pervade our approach to him. Then comes the heart's repose.

When we address God as "Dear God" or abruptly offer a prayer to him, are we guilty of too great familiarity or irreverence?

O GOD, we delight in the mystery of thy being and in the majesty of thy perfection. Let thy repose fill our souls. Amen.

19 THE SPIRITUALITY OF GOD

ZOROASTRIANISM

Now will I speak out: At the beginning of life
The holier Mentality said to the opposing Mentality who was
*   more hostile,*
"Neither our thoughts, doctrines, plans,

20

Beliefs, utterances, deeds,
Individualities, nor souls agree."

.   .   .   .

Now will I speak out what is the best of life:
Through Justice, O Mazda, have I discovered thee, who has cre-
ated him;
That Mazda is the father of the working Good Disposition;
And that Love, who produces good deeds, is his daughter;
And that the all-detecting Ahura is not to be deceived.

.   .   .   .

How shalt thou, O individual believer, with hymns of Love,
magnify
Him who is reputed to be Ahura Mazda for eternity;
Since through Justice and Good Disposition he has promised us
That in his realm we shall obtain Health and Immortality.

YASNA 45

Zoroaster's prophetic insight into the nature of God combines a kind of dualism with the doctrine of God's spirituality. The dualism is also spiritual, although later Zoroastrianism conceived of God and Satan as manlike beings opposed to each other. In this Gatha (Psalm) Ahura Mazda is the "holier Mentality" opposed to the unholy Mentality. This is putting the finger on God's nature as well as on man's duty. God is all goodness; in him is no compromise with evil. Zoroaster therefore demands that good people take a decisive stand in the battle against the "thoughts, doctrines, plans, beliefs, utterances, deeds, individualities, [and] souls" of the adversary, who dwells in people of ill will. Mazda is discovered through Justice, his creature; he is revealed through the "working Good Disposition," his son, and through Love, his daughter, who gives birth to good deeds. In this realm of the spirit we obtain wholeness of life (health) and immortality.

These insights of Zoroaster challenge our own spiritual maturity.

O GOD, create in us the love of wisdom, the wisdom of love, and the passion for justice, that we may live with thee whose being is inseparable from truth and goodness and right decisions. Amen.

20 GOD'S POWER AND GRACE

ISLAM

In the name of God, the Compassionate, the Merciful.
  Praise be to God, Lord of the Worlds!
  The compassionate, the merciful!
  King on the day of judgment!
  Thee only *do we worship, and to Thee do we cry for help.*
  Guide Thou us on the straight path.
  The path of those to whom Thou art gracious;
  Not of those with whom Thou art angered, nor of those who
    go astray.

KORAN 1

  Say: He is one God:
  God the everlasting!
  He begetteth not, and He is not begotten;
  And there is none like unto Him.

KORAN 112

  God! There is no god but he; the Living, the Self-subsisting; neither slumber seizeth him, nor sleep . . . he is the High, the Great!

KORAN 2:256

Muhammad was not the philosopher; he was the prophet. Here is the record of his vision and its message. That message was that God is one, eternal and unique; there is none like him. He is self-subsisting—like the Way of Taoism, which "conforms to its own nature." He is the living power of the universe. But above all, he is the compassionate, the merciful. The great modern scholar Ameer Ali sums up the Islamic idea of God: "God is the Holy, the Peaceful, the Faithful, the Guardian over His servants, the Shelterer of the orphan, the Guide of the erring, the Deliverer from every affliction, the Friend of the bereaved, the Consoler of the afflicted; in His hand is good, and He is the generous Lord, the Gracious, the Hearer, the Near-at-Hand, the Compassionate, the Merciful, the Very-forgiving, whose love for man is more tender than that of the mother-bird for her young."

When a man has experiences such as Muhammad's, we may forgive him for describing them in symbolic terms that differ from ours.

GOD BE MERCIFUL to us, that we may be humble and show thy mercy to others. May our rivalry with other faiths be in our endeavor to excel in kindness, understanding, and all other virtue. Amen.

21 THE WAY EVERLASTING

OLD TESTAMENT

Whither shall I go from thy Spirit?
  Or whither shall I flee from thy presence?
If I ascend to heaven, thou art there!
  If I make my bed in Sheol, thou art there!
If I take the wings of the morning
  and dwell in the uttermost parts of the sea,
even there thy hand shall lead me,
  and thy right hand shall hold me.

  . . . .

Search me, O God, and know my heart!
  Try me and know my thoughts!

And see if there be any wicked way in me,
and lead me in the way everlasting!

PSALM 139:7-10, 23-24

This highly figurative language does not portray a desire
to escape from the presence of God. It merely exclaims that
his spirit is everywhere, in all possible human experiences—
even in death itself (Sheol). In all places and in all experiences "thy hand shall lead me, and thy right hand shall
hold me." But there must be a pure heart for divine companionship. Purity of heart, said Kierkegaard, is "to will
only one thing, genuinely to will the Good, as an individual,
to will to hold fast to God, which things each person without exception is capable of doing; this is what unites."
This calls for a pause in order to avoid superficiality, in
order to gain depth and truth and goodness. "To pause is
to deepen oneself in inwardness." This is what it means to
be led "in the way everlasting."

When we examine our hearts humbly in order to gain
depth of wisdom, goodness, and love, we have in that very
act opened the door to God's presence.

"FATHER IN HEAVEN! What is a man without Thee!
What is all that he knows, vast accumulation though it
be, but a chipped fragment if he does not know Thee!
What is all his striving, could it even encompass the
world, but a half-finished work if he does not know Thee:
Thee the One, who art all!" Amen.

In the beginning was the Word, and the Word was with God, and the Word was God. He was in the beginning with God; all things were made through him, and without him was not anything made that was made. In him was life, and the life was the light of men. The light shines in the darkness, and the darkness has not overcome it.

And the Word became flesh and dwelt among us, full of grace and truth. JOHN 1:1-5, 14

The hour is coming, and now is, when the true worshipers will worship the Father in spirit and truth, for such the Father seeks to worship him. God is spirit, and those who worship him must worship in spirit and truth. JOHN 4:23-24

Here is one of the greatest passages of all scriptures. God is said to be the Word (Logos). Words are both the embodiment of wisdom and the expression of wisdom. As the universal Word, God is all truth and all wisdom, absolute and unaffected by human misunderstanding and ignorance. But a word is also intended to reveal wisdom to other people. Unfortunately, when men try to understand God's wisdom, they are likely to misunderstand, as happens so often in ordinary exchange of words. John insisted that Jesus, in his life and teachings, revealed the wisdom that is God. In a sense, Jesus *was* the Word which he revealed, as words are identical with the wisdom which they express. Following up this thought, Jesus himself told the Samaritan woman that "God is spirit, and those who worship him must worship in spirit and truth." Spirit means values, such as wisdom, truth, and goodness. Such is the nature of God, with power.

Jesus challenged his disciples to be godlike by striving for the perfection that is God: "You, therefore, must be perfect, as your heavenly Father is perfect."

O God, help us to strive for nothing less than the divine image of thy perfect wisdom and love. Amen.

23 GOD IS LOVE

Beloved, let us love one another; for love is of God, and he who loves is born of God and knows God. He who does not love does not know God; for God is love. . . . No man has ever seen God; if we love one another, God abides in us and his love is perfected in us. . . . God is love, and he who abides in love abides in God, and God abides in him. In this is love perfected with us, that we may have confidence for the day of judgment, because as he is so are we in this world. There is no fear in love, but perfect love casts out fear. For fear has to do with punishment, and he who fears is not perfected in love. We love, because he first loved us. If any one says, "I love God," and hates his brother, he is a liar; for he who does not love his brother whom he has seen, cannot love God whom he has not seen. And this commandment we have from him, that he who loves God should love his brother also.   1 JOHN 4:7-8, 12, 16-21

He who takes the Christian scriptures literally should begin with this passage. The writer makes it emphatic that God is identical with *agape*—outgoing, unselfish love. The only way to have satisfactory relations with God is to love both God and our fellow men. God's love for men is without limitation, and we join with God only as we join in loving our brother. We respond to the love that is God only when we love our fellow men. Perhaps it oversimplifies the case to say that God is *agape*—nothing less, and nothing more. But at least we may be sure that perfect love is of the essence of God.

God is certainly more than our collective human love, weak and imperfect as it is. Yet our failure to love without limit may limit God.

> "Love divine, all loves excelling,
>
> .   .   .   .
>
> Fix in us thy humble dwelling." Amen.

24 THE SHRINE OF THE HEART

SIKHISM

Whither shall I go, Sir? I am happy at home.
My heart will not go with me; it hath become a cripple.
One day I did have an inclination to go;
I ground sandal, took distilled aloe wood and many perfumes,
And was proceeding to worship God in a temple,
When my spiritual guide showed me God in my heart.

GRANTH

Written by the prophet-poet Ramananda about 1400 A.D., these verses found their way into the Bible of Sikhism two hundred years later. Contrary to the belief of many that God was to be found in certain spots or in certain traditions rather than in others, Ramananda asserted that God is to be found in the heart. It is useless to go to the temple seeking God unless God is already in the heart. Worth noting is the fact that Ramananda did worship in temples. Clearly he regarded the experience as refreshing, provided that one first knows God in the heart.

Insincerity of motive in public service may, indeed, stand in the way of a genuine experience of God's presence.

O God, help us to shake off all pretense of belief and false tradition when they are unsupported by the realities of experience. Enable us to make a fresh discovery of the meaning of God in the experience of the heart. And may the shrine of our spirits be more pure than any earthly temple. Amen.

25 GOD IN THE FLESH

BUDDHISM

He who seeth the Dharma, seeth me; he who seeth me, seeth the Dharma. SAMYUTTA 22.87

Modern scholars understand the Buddha to have taught that God is not some abstract, faraway being, but the inner law of this universe of pulsating life. Dharma is Law. The Buddha thus identified himself with an immanent God, or Law, comparable with the Greek Logos, the Word of John 1:1. His was not an abstract identity, but an identity of purpose, spirit, and attitude through love of the wise, the universal, and the eternal. His later followers often took this literally and made him a God. The man Buddha was simply a mystic who had had an experience of divine wisdom and fearlessly identified himself with that wisdom. He was not afraid to commit himself to it as a way of life. Jesus' identification of himself with God was more exclusive than Buddha's, according to John's Gospel (14:6, 9-10).

If God is indeed a kind of Dharma-Law, as Buddha

seems to have conceived him to be, it is difficult to deny that God revealed himself to people in other traditions than our own.

O GOD, may we feel a spiritual unity with the people of all lands through all the prophets of the great traditions. May we find joy in our realization of man's unity in thyself. Amen.

26 GOD IN OUR LIVES

The Buddhas in the innumerable Buddha-lands
Are naught but the Buddha within our own soul;
The Golden Lotus, as multitudinous as the drops
Of ocean water, is living in our body. . . .
In realizing all this every one shall attain
The glories of being, even in this corporeal life.

These are the words of Kukai, or Kobo Daishi (774-835 A.D.), one of the founders of Shingon Japanese Buddhism. His was a mysticism which regarded all the tales of the Buddhas as myths having only one meaning, namely, that the true God dwelt deep within our hearts. For him heaven was a present experience. The essence of that heavenly experience was universal truth, wisdom, mercy, and love, which unite us with our fellow men. The Golden Lotus is the flower which grows beautifully amid repulsive surroundings, thus symbolizing the enlightened one who lives beautifully regardless of circumstances. Buddhists, of course, regard the Buddha as the perfect example of the Golden Lotus.

Any great tradition needs a succession of prophets, such as Kukai for Buddhism, to keep it vital and fresh.

O GOD, speak to us through the ministry of thy prophets everywhere and in all times, that we may know how great thou art. May we recognize thy presence in the hearts of others as in our own. Amen.

27 THE PEACE OF GOD

HINDUISM

Atman, smaller than the small, greater than the great, is hidden in the hearts of all living creatures. A man who is free from desires beholds the majesty of the Self through tranquility of the senses and the mind and becomes free from grief.

KATHA UPANISHAD 1.2.20

This Atman cannot be attained by the study of the Vedas, or by intelligence, or by much hearing of sacred books. It is attained by him alone whom It chooses. To such a one Atman reveals Its own form.   KATHA UPANISHAD 1.2.23

Atman is the word used to refer to Brahman as he is reflected in the spirit of man. Atman is the Universal Self. Though God's nature transcends the powers of reason and sense, yet we can know him in our hearts. But we must take a quiet moment and look within in order to find him. Even then, God's self-revelation is not mechanically produced but comes through his grace and love. The vision frees us from grief and anxiety, says the writer of the Katha Upanishad. Christian mystics agree:

I ask no dream, no prophet ecstasies,
  No sudden rending of the veil of clay,

No angel visitant, no opening skies;
But take the dimness of my soul away.

God's presence, like sincere friendship, cannot be bought. It may be said that God is present even when we know it not. What we need is to remove our dimness of soul so that we may perceive him both in ourselves and in others.

O GOD, may thy love lead us in the path to that spiritual reality which links us with a higher world, binds us to our fellow man, and frees us from grief. We desire thy peace and benediction. Amen.

28 A MYSTIC'S RESPONSE

OLD TESTAMENT

And the angel of the Lord appeared to him in a flame of fire out of the midst of a bush; and he looked, and lo, the bush was burning, yet it was not consumed. And Moses said, "I will turn aside and see this great sight, why the bush is not burnt." When the Lord saw that he turned aside to see, God called to him out of the bush, "Moses, Moses!" And he said, "Here am I." Then he said, "Do not come near; put off your shoes from your feet, for the place on which you are standing is holy ground." And he said, "I am the God of your father, the God of Abraham, the God of Isaac, and the God of Jacob." And Moses hid his face, for he was afraid to look at God.

Then the Lord said, "I have seen the affliction of my people who are in Egypt, and have heard their cry because of their taskmasters; I know their sufferings, and I have come down to deliver them out of the hand of the Egyptians. . . . Come, I will send you to Pharaoh that you may bring forth my people. . . .
EXODUS 3:2-8, 10

31

This reminds us of the vision of Isaiah which ended with the challenge of a holy Lord, "Whom shall I send, and who will go for us?" The mystic's response was, "Here am I! Send me" (Isaiah 6:8). No mystic has ever had a vision of God without sensing an ensuing responsibility. In the case of Moses, his awareness of the plight of his Hebrew brethren in Egypt vivified his need of divine aid. But the divine aid, when it came, was channeled through him. His sensitivity to the presence and purpose of God is given universal meaning in the words of Elizabeth Barrett Browning:

> Earth's crammed with heaven,
> And every common bush afire with God;
> But only he who sees takes off his shoes—
> The rest sit round it and pluck blackberries.

People with a deep sense of social responsibility are the ones most likely to have visions even today.

O GOD, may we be true to the visions that we do have of truth and duty, instead of expecting more dramatic ones. Amen.

29 THE STILL SMALL VOICE

OLD TESTAMENT

And behold, the Lord passed by, and a great and strong wind rent the mountains, and broke in pieces the rocks before the Lord, but the Lord was not in the wind; and after the wind an earthquake, but the Lord was not in the earthquake; and after the earthquake a fire, but the Lord was not in the fire; and after the fire a still small voice. And when Elijah heard it, he wrapped

*his face in his mantle and went out and stood at the entrance
of the cave.* 1 KINGS 19:11-13

God does speak to people today, as he did to prophets
of old. But his word is likely to be not in the strong wind,
nor in the earthquake, nor in the fire, but in the still small
voice. Whenever we perceive the clear truth or the duty of
love and service, we have heard the voice of God. As
James Russell Lowell wrote:

God is not dumb, that He should speak no more;
    If thou hast wanderings in the wilderness
And find'st not Sinai, 'tis thy soul is poor;
    There towers the Mountain of the Voice no less,
Which whoso seeks shall find; but he who bends,
Intent on manna still and mortal ends,
    Sees it not, neither hears its thundered lore.

Slowly the Bible of the race is writ,
    And not on paper leaves nor leaves of stone;
Each age, each kindred, adds a verse to it,
    Texts of despair and hope, of joy or moan.
While swings the sea, while mists the mountains shroud,
While thunder's surges burst on cliff of cloud,
    Still at the prophets' feet the nations sit.

All who hear God's voice may be his prophet in some
small way.

O GOD, may we ever be sensitive to the still small voice
as it speaks quietly of simple truth and love. Amen.

O the great Way o'er flows
And spreads on every side!
All being comes from it;
No creature is denied.
But having called them forth,
It calls not one its own.
It feeds and clothes them all
And will not be their lord.

TAO TÊ CHING 34

The idea of God's gracious kindness to man and nature is common to all religions. Here we find it in the words of Lao Tzu, legendary founder of Chinese Taoism. The same idea is expressed by his contemporary Mo Tzu: "Heaven loves the whole world universally. Everything is prepared for the good man. Even the tip of a hair is the work of Heaven. Substantial may be said of the benefits that are enjoyed by man. Yet there is no service in return." Or in the words of Jesus: "Love your enemies, and do good, and lend, expecting nothing in return; and your reward will be great, and you will be sons of the Most High; for he is kind to the ungrateful and the selfish. Be merciful, even as your Father is merciful."

Why should it be thought that a good God would ever want to bring evil on his creatures—especially if we sin through ignorance of what is best?

O GOD, may thy grace so fill our lives that we may be gracious even to our enemies. Amen.

31 GOD IS MY SHEPHERD

The Lord is my shepherd, I shall not want;
* he makes me lie down in green pastures.*
He leads me beside still waters,
* he restores my soul.*
He leads me in paths of righteousness
* for his name's sake.*

Even though I walk through the valley of the
*   shadow of death,*
* I fear no evil;*
for thou art with me;
* thy rod and thy staff,*
* they comfort me.*

Thou preparest a table before me
* in the presence of my enemies;*
thou anointest my head with oil,
* my cup overflows.*
Surely goodness and mercy shall follow me
* all the days of my life;*
and I shall dwell in the house of the Lord
* for ever.*

PSALM 23

Since God is the very essence of wisdom, goodness, and love, vivified in some way beyond the power of our prosaic, logical minds to comprehend, then God's guidance means the leadership of wisdom, goodness, and love. Following in his ways of wisdom brings peace and contentment. Walking in paths of righteousness calls for some self-discipline and effort. Love makes possible the fraternal feasts even in the presence of those who hate us. Living in the house of such a God is a joy for ever.

This comforting psalm reminds us that one of the proper functions of religion is to comfort and strengthen us.

O GOD, may we be so faithful to the divine leadership that we need fear no evil. May our confidence be in righteousness. Amen.

32 GOD'S PITY

OLD TESTAMENT

Bless the Lord, O my soul;
and all that is within me, bless his holy name!
Bless the Lord, O my soul,
and forget not all his benefits,
who forgives all your iniquity,
who heals all your diseases,
who redeems your life from the Pit,
who crowns you with steadfast love and mercy,
who satisfies you with good as long as you live
so that your youth is renewed like the eagle's.

. . . .

As a father pities his children,
so the Lord pities those who fear him.
For he knows our frame;
he remembers that we are dust.

PSALM 103:1-5, 13-14

It is man's destiny to rule earth, sea, and air. His is a proud position on this planet, but he holds it for only a day. His frame is clay; his vision is God. Man is tantalized and lured on by the vistas of perfection in self and society, just as he looks out on a universe that stretches into countless light-years. Although he enjoys the proudest position on earth, he pities himself because he has time for a mere glimpse of the glory that is God's alone. But let us not forget that it is wonderful to share the glory of the eternal even for a day and that while we live, God satisfies us with goodness and continually renews the joy of our youth. And our hope is for immortality.

Is God's pity really our pity for ourselves against a background of the perfection that is God's? If we are in God's spiritual image, we may argue that man's pity for man forms an important part of God's redemptive love for man.

GOD GIVE US FAITH in our divine kinship and acceptance of our human situation. Amen.

33 GOD'S OTHER CHILDREN

OLD TESTAMENT

Jonah was exceedingly glad because of the plant. But when dawn came up the next day, God appointed a worm which attacked the plant, so that it withered. When the sun rose, God appointed a sultry east wind, and the sun beat upon the head of Jonah so that he was faint; and he asked that he might die, and said, "It is better for me to die than to live." But God said to Jonah, "Do you do well to be angry for the plant?" And he said, "I do well to be angry, angry enough to die." And the Lord said, "You pity the plant, for which you did not labor, nor did you make it grow, which came into being in a night, and perished in a night. And should not I pity Nineveh, that great city, in which

37

*there are more than a hundred and twenty thousand persons
who do not know their right hand from their left, and also
much cattle?"*   JONAH 4:6-11

The author of the book of Jonah took these drastic
means to show his fellow Jews that God loved all men
equally. God's message to the Ninevites was that they must
repent or perish. When they repented, Jonah was angry for
he thought they deserved to perish. He knew their wickedness. So did God, who knew the Jews' as well. The message
of the story falls today on unperceiving hearts. All men
seek God. God loves them all and seeks them equally.
When some seek all the privileges of life, denying them to
others, are they better than Jonah?

God is more likely to be truly our father when we do
not claim him as our exclusive possession.

O GOD, help us to show good will and genuine respect to
the people of all races and creeds and thus prove that we
are thy children. Amen.

34 GOD'S FRIENDS

NEW TESTAMENT

*Now the tax collectors and sinners were all drawing near to
hear him. And the Pharisees and the scribes murmured, saying,
"This man receives sinners and eats with them."*

*So he told them this parable: "What man of you, having a
hundred sheep, if he has lost one of them, does not leave the
ninety-nine in the wilderness, and go after the one which is lost,
until he finds it? And when he has found it, he lays it on his
shoulders, rejoicing. And when he comes home, he calls together
his friends and his neighbors, saying to them, 'Rejoice with me,*

for I have found my sheep which was lost.' Even so, I tell you,
there will be more joy in heaven over one sinner who repents
than over ninety-nine righteous persons who need no repentance."

In the parable God is likened to a shepherd seeking his
lost sheep. In carrying on the work of God, Jesus made
friends with sinners and saints alike. His purpose was to
bring all into a universal fellowship. We are inclined to
choose our friends on a different principle. Perhaps that is
because we are more dependent on the influence of our
friends in forming our own characters. But our goal should
be the same as that of Jesus—to bring all into a universal
fellowship. One who has a strong character can form friendships with all kinds of people, looking always for the broad
human qualities in each one. Thus he will not think of
himself as "holier than thou."

To adopt the principle that "God's friends are my
friends" would quicken and enrich our human relationships
significantly.

O GOD, may our motives in friendship be worthy of our
divine calling. Amen.

35 FAITH WHILE SUFFERING

The potter does not test cracked vessels, for he need only
knock upon them once and they break; but if he test sound ves-
sels, he can knock upon them many times without their breaking.
Similarly the Holy One, blessed be he, does not try the wicked
but the righteous; as it is said, "The Lord trieth the righteous,"
and it is written, "God did test Abraham." Parable of a house-

*holder who had two cows, one strong and the other weak. Upon
which of them does he place the yoke? Surely upon the strong.
In the same manner God tests the righteous.* TALMUD

This reasoning of the ancient Jewish rabbis is not absolute, but only by analogy. It is intended to console people
who are suffering. Certain it is that those who are suffering need consolation. The typical complaint of those who
suffer is, "Why should this happen to me?" Usually there
is no satisfactory answer. If it is really God who brings the
suffering upon us, then the answer of the rabbis is perhaps
as good as one can find. And if it provides any real consolation, then it is a worthy answer to that extent. After all,
one may as well accept the suffering if it cannot be avoided.
Complaining about it does no more good than trying to
understand it. And it is true that nobility of soul can result
from testing patiently borne.

It is really hard to believe that God wills evil at all.

O GOD, if it be not thy will that we should suffer, nevertheless when pain and sorrow come, may we learn to accept our human lot with cheer. Amen.

36 TRIALS OF THE SOUL

OLD TESTAMENT

*My face is red with weeping,
 and on my eyelids is deep darkness;
although there is no violence in my hands,
 and my prayer is pure.*

JOB 16:16-17

*Behold, I cry out, "Violence!" but I am not answered;
 I call aloud, but there is no justice.*

He has walled up my way, so that I cannot pass,
  and he has set darkness upon my paths.
He has stripped from me my glory,
  and taken the crown from my head.
He breaks me down on every side, and I am gone,
  and my hope has he pulled up like a tree.
He has kindled his wrath against me,
  and counts me as his adversary.

JOB 19:7-11

Consolation fails in times of great suffering, as in the case of Job when he lost family, health, and possessions. Two thoughts made him especially bitter. One was that he had been so happy before; now by contrast his suffering seemed especially terrible. The other was that he regarded suffering as divine punishment, and he rebelled against a God who would treat him so unjustly. When great happiness is followed sharply by great suffering, all that we can do is to be grateful that we have had at least a time of happiness. But as for blaming God, this thought needs correction. As Spinoza said, taking refuge in "the will of God (is) the sanctuary of ignorance." If a stone falls from a roof and kills a passer-by, "the event is due to the facts that the wind was blowing, and the man was walking that way." Said Mencius, "He who has the true idea of what is heaven's appointment will not stand beneath a precipitous wall."

It is true that our lives are in God's hands—though not in the sense that God is a manlike being who is subject to human passions and arbitrary behavior.

O GOD, may we be thy ministering servants by refusing to bring evil on any human being and by trying to ease suffering wherever we can. Amen.

Why do the wicked live,
and reach old age, and grow mighty in power?
Their children are established in their presence,
and their offspring before their eyes.

. . . .

They send forth their little ones like a flock,
and their children dance.
They sing to the tambourine and the lyre,
and rejoice to the sound of the pipe.
They spend their days in prosperity,
and in peace they go down to Sheol.
They say to God, "Depart from us!
We do not desire the knowledge of thy ways.
What is the Almighty, that we should serve him?
And what profit do we get if we pray to him?"

. . . .

How then will you comfort me with empty nothings?
There is nothing left of your answers but falsehood.

JOB 21:7-8, 11-15, 34

Job found fault with the justice of God's administration of human affairs. The good died young while the wicked lived to old age. Their children lived gay lives and enjoyed prosperity. The wicked showed no reverence for God. Yet God did not punish them. Job's assumption was that goodness ought to be rewarded by success and happiness, whereas wickedness should result in suffering. Plato's thesis was that goodness is its own reward. If success and health and family and friends are added, that is just so much more to be grateful for. We really should feel sorry for the wicked because their happiness is superficial; they do not

understand the beauty of goodness. Yet we can hardly
blame people like Job for feeling that God had forsaken
them.

Socrates, unjustly condemned, would never have traded
places with the wicked, even for the purpose of escaping
death.

O God, give us first health of soul and peace of mind, and
may we be worthy of the physical health and prosperity
that we so often take for granted. Amen.

38   GOD'S MAJESTY

OLD TESTAMENT

Where were you when I laid the foundation of the earth?
   Tell me, if you have understanding.
Who determined its measurements—surely you know!
   Or who stretched the line upon it?
On what were its bases sunk,
   or who laid its cornerstone,
when the morning stars sang together,
   and all the sons of God shouted for joy?
Or who shut in the sea with doors,
   when it burst forth from the womb;
when I made clouds its garment,
   and thick darkness its swaddling band.

. . . .

Has the rain a father,
   or who has begotten the drops of dew?
From whose womb did the ice come forth,
   and who has given birth to the hoarfrost of heaven?
The waters become hard like stone,
   and the face of the deep is frozen.

43

Can you bind the chains of the Pleiades,
or loose the cords of Orion?

.   .   .   .

Will you even put me in the wrong?
Will you condemn me that you may be justified?
JOB 38:4-9, 28-31; 40:8

One who doubted honestly, came honestly to believe. Tennyson perceived that without the doubt there could have been no depth of faith:

> You say, but with no touch of scorn,
>   Sweet-hearted, you, whose light-blue eyes
>   Are tender over drowning flies,
> You tell me, doubt is Devil-born.
>
> I know not: one indeed I knew
>   In many a subtle question versed,
>   Who touch'd a jarring lyre at first
> But ever strove to make it true:
>
> Perplext in faith, but pure in deeds,
>   At last he beat his music out.
>   There lives more faith in honest doubt,
> Believe me, than in half the creeds.

Job never did find the answers to his doubts. Yet in view of the majesty of God's creation, he felt that it behooved him to doubt his doubts concerning the justice of God. The problem of the injustice of life is perhaps no greater than that of the origin of being.

O GOD, may we cling to the simple truths of life and build a worthy faith sincerely. Amen.

All things are full of weariness;
a man cannot utter it;
the eye is not satisfied with seeing,
nor the ear filled with hearing.
What has been is what will be,
and what has been done is what will be done;
and there is nothing new under the sun.
Is there a thing of which it is said,
"See, this is new"?
It has been already,
in the ages before us.
There is no remembrance of former things,
nor will there be any remembrance
of later things yet to happen
among those who come after.

ECCLESIASTES 1:8-11

Here is a man who is fed up with life. He demands
novelty and excitement, but he has experienced so many
things so often that all now seem tame. He turns his
thought inward in sickly self-analysis. What he says is
largely true, that the same things happen over and over
again in human experience. Babies are born, go through the
same cycles of development, mature and marry, have
children who go through the same cycles as their parents,
and all grow old and die. Each generation remembers some
of the achievements of the preceding generation. But let
another generation pass, and nothing is remembered.

The trouble with this whole complaint is that happiness

is being sought through selfish motive. The outward look of selfless service leads to optimism.

GOD HELP US to find life good by making it good for others. Amen.

40 THE VARIETY OF LIFE

OLD TESTAMENT

For everything there is a season, and a time for every matter under heaven:
a time to be born, and a time to die;
a time to plant, and a time to pluck up what is planted;
a time to kill, and a time to heal;
a time to break down, and a time to build up;
a time to weep, and a time to laugh;
a time to mourn, and a time to dance;
a time to cast away stones, and a time to gather stones together;
a time to embrace, and a time to refrain from embracing;
a time to seek, and a time to lose;
a time to keep, and a time to cast away;
a time to rend, and a time to sew;
a time to keep silence, and a time to speak;
a time to love, and a time to hate;
a time for war, and a time for peace.
What gain has the worker from his toil?

ECCLESIASTES 3:1-9

Some see rhythm in the variety of life and find it good. But the author of Ecclesiastes looked at it dimly. What is the use of being born if later we must die? Why plant if we must pluck up? War and peace, love and hate, seeking and losing, laughing and weeping, killing and healing— these opposites of conduct only proved to him that life had no real meaning or principle. "What gain has the worker from his toil?" But we might look at it another way. Since life and death are two parts of the same process, we can understand that the privilege of being born involves the inevitability of death; the capacity for laughter is really the same as that for weeping; so also for love and hate, seeking and losing, killing and healing, war and peace.

> The world is so full of a number of things,
> I'm sure we should all be as happy as kings.

No doubt life has more variety than we like in some respects, and we should try to eliminate the destructive elements so far as possible. But life itself is fundamentally good.

When the opposites of life strike us in close succession, there is some small consolation in understanding and accepting the human situation.

GOD, HELP US to minimize our complaints and praise thee for the joy of living. Amen.

41 ESCAPE FROM PESSIMISM

HINDUISM

A man should not hate any living creature. Let him be friendly and compassionate to all. He must free himself from the delusion of the "I" and "mine." He must accept pleasure and pain with equal tranquility. He must be forgiving, ever-contented, self-controlled, united constantly with me in his meditation. His re-

solve must be unshakable. He must be dedicated to me in intellect and mind. Such a devotee is dear to me. BHAGAVAD-GITA 12.13, 14

This passage from the "New Testament" of Hinduism breathes the spirit of resignation and contentment in a universe where anything can happen. Love, forgiveness, self-control, constancy, and mystic sensitivity are the qualities of character sought. Divine companionship is the source of strength.

It is sometimes said that resignation and contentment discourage achievement. Perhaps. Yet contentment is of great value in true perspective.

SPIRIT OF TRUTH, so guide us that our self-analysis may reveal any hidden feelings of hatred, for we would find companionship with thee through friendship and compassion for all. Amen.

42 HOW TO PLAN

BUDDHISM

"Here shall I pass the monsoon; here shall I dwell during winter and summer." Thus reflects the fool, but knows not the dangers to his life. DHAMMAPADA 286

Like the rich fool of Luke 12:15-21, we tend to forget that life is short. We sometimes behave as if our human lives would never end. We make plans as if there were no danger of death coming suddenly. Life goes on precariously.

An old horse, notwithstanding, thinks himself a colt,
And has no regard for the future.

SHIH CHING

The wise man plans tentatively. The possibility of sudden death must always be taken into account. The philosophy of Existentialism is based upon this insight among others. We are moments of freedom in the universe. Every decision we make is crucial and irrevocable. We never know enough to make a completely rational decision, but we cannot postpone the decision long enough to get the requisite knowledge. We must do our best and leave the outcome to God.

It may be unwholesome to dwell upon the brevity of life. But it is unwise to ignore it.

ETERNAL GOD, help us to face life realistically, courageously, and with steady faith. May we shun the fool's paradise while we try to build the kingdom of heaven. Amen.

43 HUMAN SYMPATHY

CONFUCIANISM

If men suddenly see a child about to fall into a well, they will without exception experience a feeling of alarm and distress. They will feel so, not as a ground on which they may seek the praise of their neighbors and friends, nor from a dislike to the reputation of having been unmoved by such a thing.

From this case we may perceive that the feeling of commiseration is essential to man. . . . The feeling of commiseration is the principle of benevolence.   MENCIUS 2

It is all too easy to lose faith in human nature. If man is half angel and half beast, it seems sometimes that the beast overcomes the angel too easily. Nevertheless, a careful look reveals nobility in human nature. A stranger looks

49

confused (as he is) in a New York subway station, and several people offer to help him. Even the hardest of men find softening sympathy working in their hearts. One can overstress the goodness of human nature, as probably Mencius did. Good and bad are both there. That is one of the tensions that make up man's life.

Perhaps the pessimists should be more optimistic about man, and the optimists more cautious.

SPIRIT OF LOVE, help us always to look for the best in men and to help them to be their best. Amen.

44 THE IMAGE OF GOD

OLD TESTAMENT

Then God said, "Let us make man in our image, after our likeness; and let them have dominion over the fish of the sea, and over the birds of the air, and over the cattle, and over all the earth, and over every creeping thing that creeps upon the earth." So God created man in his own image, in the image of God he created him; male and female he created them. And God blessed them, and God said to them, "Be fruitful and multiply, and fill the earth and subdue it; and have dominion over the fish of the sea and over the birds of the air and over every living thing that moves upon the earth." . . . And God saw everything that he had made, and behold, it was very good. GENESIS 1:26-28, 31

The Westminster Shorter Catechism explains that man is in the image of God "in knowledge, righteousness, and holiness, with dominion over the creatures." The divine creation was incomplete until an organism came into existence bearing a consciousness of values. If "God is spirit," certainly there is no better meaning to assign to spirit than identity with such values as truth, goodness, and love. Man reflects this divine image in his inmost nature. He reflects God's power in his control over creatures and over natural resources, with tender regard for their conservation.

The mystery of man's soul united with his body seems no greater than the mystery of the values of perfection united in God.

SPIRIT OF GOD, be perfected in us this day and every day. Amen.

45 THE LIGHT OF GOODNESS

BUDDHISM

The good shine from afar like the Himalayan range, while those lacking virtue vanish unseen, as arrows shot in a dark night. DHAMMAPADA 304

It is hard to conceive of a greater contrast than that here suggested. Mount Everest in the Himalayas rises to over twenty-nine thousand feet above sea level and is closely rivaled by others in the same range. Their sublime beauty can be seen for many miles, dominating the whole area as they do. In contrast, arrows shot in a dark night are seen not at all or at most for only a chance instant. So are the nonvirtuous in contrast with the virtuous, whose lives are lustrous with beauty and good influence. There is a peacefulness and stability in the inner life of the virtuous and an imposing attractiveness to those who observe their goodness.

Notoriety is fleeting and ministers only to conceit. The

virtuous shun fame, although their goodness multiplies around them.

GOD OF PERFECTION, may we recognize the kinship between the great prophets and common people of outstanding virtue today and be inspired by both. Amen.

46   WHENCE COMES DESTRUCTION?

CONFUCIANISM

A man must first despise himself, and then others will despise him. A family must first destroy itself, and then others will destroy it. A kingdom must first smite itself, and then others will smite it.   MENCIUS 4

How often do we blame others for those things for which we are primarily responsible! Actually, there is not much point in placing the blame, except that by so doing we may be able to avoid similar misfortunes in the future. We only compound our troubles by blaming those who are not responsible. Moreover, if we are really the ones who are at fault, the frank acknowledgment of that fact will go a long way toward a remedy. If others do not think highly of us, perhaps it is truly because we do not respect ourselves highly. There may be reason for our lack of self-respect. In any case, strength comes from within through proper reconstruction and planning. This is as true of groups and nations as of individuals. It is one of the theses of Arnold Toynbee and is generally sound.

Repentance must precede self-respect; reconstruction accompanies it.

LORD OF OUR LIVES, make us keen to perceive any weakness within us or in our associations. May we be humble in repentance and effort. Amen.

47 GENESIS OF SIN

> *If one*
> *Ponders on objects of the sense, there springs*
> *Attraction; from attraction grows desire,*
> *Desire flames to fierce passion, passion breeds*
> *Recklessness; then the memory—all betrayed—*
> *Lets noble purpose go, and saps the mind,*
> *Till purpose, mind, and man are all undone.*
>
> BHAGAVAD-GITA 2

This is one of the passages quoted by Gandhi in his *Autobiography* in order to illustrate how the Gita had influenced him. He continues, "The book struck me as one of priceless worth. The impression has ever since been growing on me with the result that I regard it today as the book par excellence for the knowledge of Truth. It has afforded me invaluable help in my moments of gloom. . . . It was only after some years that it became a book of daily reading." The passage from the Gita forms a blueprint of self-destruction. If through such analysis we come to realize how sin destroys our integrity and normal good purpose, then we should be better able to avoid the same path in the future. We need to develop techniques in living the good life, just as in any other kind of undertaking.

Gandhi's initial assumption is that the contemplated object of sense is of a type that is spiritually destructive.

Certainly his analysis applies only to objects in that category.

GOD OF POWER, make us vigilant in the struggle for complete moral victory, lest we be defeated by neglect. Amen.

48 CIVILIZATION AND PIETY

ZOROASTRIANISM

*O Ahura, I ask thee what shall be the punishments of those who
. . . cannot make their living
Without violence to cattle and to . . . (herdsmen).
O Mazda Ahura, I ask thee whether the well-disposed man who
may strive
To improve the houses, the villages, the clans and the provinces,
through Justice,
Whether he may at all become a being like unto thee; if so,
when he shall arise unto this likeness and what deeds he shall
do to become such.*

. . . .

*From the resources of his innate glory, Ahura Mazda shall grant
sustained communion
And fullness of Health, and Immortality, and of Justice and of
Power and Good Disposition
To whomsoever is a friend to Ahura Mazda in mind and deeds.
The man who is well-disposed, understands this as clearly as does
Mazda, who knows with the divine Disposition.*

YASNA 31

The special insight of Zoroaster in this Gatha was that piety involves a commitment to the values of civilization. In his day that meant armed resistance to the nomadic raiders from the north. In our day it means organized resistance to international lawlessness. Worshiping God in our little sanctuaries is well and good. But it is not enough. Godliness requires that we join together aggressively "to improve the houses, the villages, the clans and the provinces, through justice." Only then comes "fullness of Health, and Immortality, and of Justice and of Power and Good Disposition to whomsoever is a friend to Ahura Mazda in mind and deeds." The capitalized nouns are the angels through whom God makes himself known to us. Through them, in turn, we make God real in civilization.

Zoroaster's land faced perils which seem small compared with those confronting us today. Greater effort is now required.

GOD OF LIGHT, enlighten us with the sense of thy justice and good will. Give us the moral strength to triumph over the evils facing us today. Amen.

49 SIN AND SLAVERY

ISLAM

A king said to a Shaikh in conversation, "Ask me for something in the way of a gift."

The Shaikh said, "Are you not ashamed to speak so to me? Be above this. I have two slaves, and despicable they are; but those two are rulers and lords over you."

The king said, "What are those two? This is an error."

He replied, "The one is 'anger' and the other 'sensuality.'"

THE MASNAVI 2

The scripture is the work of a Sufi poet, Jalalu 'D-Din Rumi, founder of the Order of Maulavi Darvishes in the thirteenth century, in Iran. He well realized that such passions as anger and sensuality can enslave the spirit of

55

man and prevent him from realizing his God-given potentialities. Many of us who are not habitual slaves to anger and sensuality may yet at times let them get the better of us. It is possible for our passions to ruin our lives simply by gaining control over our judgment for one crucial moment. A kingdom can fall through the loss of a single battle. That is why it is important for us to practice conscious control over our passions at all times.

The emotional life is not intrinsically bad, but it needs to be governed by the whole man through wisdom and purity of heart.

God FREE OUR SOULS from all enslavement and make us vigilant in the governance of our lives. May we avoid self-deception as we strive to achieve the best. Amen.

50 WILLING GOD'S WILL

JUDAISM

May . . . no hatred against us . . . enter the heart of any man nor hatred of any man enter our heart; (may) no envy of us enter the heart of any man nor envy of any man enter our heart; may thy Torah be our occupation all the days of our life. . . .

Do thou unite our hearts in the fear of thy Name; keep us far from whatever is hateful to thee; bring us near to all that thou lovest, and do justly with us for the sake of thy Name.

. . . Thou hast created us to perform thy will and so we are bound to do. Such is thy desire and such is our desire, too; but what impedes us? . . . (The evil impulse.) It is revealed and known before thee that we have not the strength to resist it; may

*it therefore be acceptable before thee, O Lord my God and God
of my fathers, that thou cause it to cease from upon us and subdue it so that we may do thy will as our will with a perfect heart.*

TALMUD

These three prayers from the Talmud are especially
beautiful in word and sentiment. The first brands envy and
hate as enemies of the good life and represents the Law as
the path of righteousness. The second hopes that we may
hate what God hates and love what he loves. The third
laments that evil impulse steals into us so that without
reflection we stray from God's will. The perfect heart is
that which has learned habitually to will God's will. God's
law and wisdom must triumph over the momentary impulses of our hearts if we are to succeed in living the life
of the spirit.

Prayer can be an empty formality. But when we pray
sincerely to be delivered from envy and hatred, half the
battle is already won.

GOD OF LOVE, may we will to do only those things which
draw mankind together in peace and righteousness. Amen.

51 THE WAGES OF SIN

OLD TESTAMENT

*And the Lord God commanded the man, saying, "You may
freely eat of every tree of the garden; but of the tree of the
knowledge of good and evil you shall not eat, for in the day that
you eat of it you shall die."*

.   .   .   .

*When the woman saw that the tree was good for food, and
that it was a delight to the eyes, and that the tree was to be de-*

*sired to make one wise, she took of its fruit and ate; and she
also gave some to her husband, and he ate. Then the eyes of
both were opened, and they knew that they were naked; and
they sewed fig leaves together and made themselves aprons.*

*And they heard the sound of the Lord God walking in the
garden in the cool of the day, and the man and his wife hid
themselves from the presence of the Lord God among the trees
of the garden.*

. . . .

*Then the Lord God . . . drove out the man; and at the east
of the garden of Eden he placed the cherubim, and a flaming
sword which turned every way, to guard the way to the tree of
life.*   GENESIS 2:16-17; 3:6-8, 24

As a parable of sin, this passage has much value. A
prevalent view is that sin is attractive, tempting. It pic-
tures the righteous as denying themselves some of the excitement of life for the sake of dull innocence. Alas, when
sin comes to full fruition, it leads to sickness and death. If
this is true, it is the wise who understand that the good
life is really the happiest life. Actually, in a literal, prosaic
sense, it is very doubtful that physical death is the result
of plucking forbidden fruit in a pristine garden. We have
a way of interpreting primitive man's symbolism much
too naïvely. Truly, the forbidden things are made to seem
the most attractive. And foolish sin prevents us from enjoy-
ing God's communion.

If we look at sin as a wholly related act, as a wise man
should, it loses its glamor and assumes its real character as
the enemy of our truest selves.

GOD OF RIGHTEOUSNESS, give us the wisdom to resist the
temptations to momentary happiness while seeking the
permanent good. Amen.

When Chuang Tzu's wife died, Hui Tzu came to the house to join in the rites of mourning. To his surprise he found Chuang Tzu sitting with an inverted bowl on his knees, drumming upon it and singing a song. "After all," said Hui Tzu, "she lived with you, brought up your children, grew old along with you. That you should not mourn for her is bad enough; but to let your friends find you drumming and singing—that is going too far!" "You misjudge me," said Chuang Tzu. "When she died, I was in despair, as any man well might be. But soon, pondering on what had happened, I told myself that in death no strange new fate befalls us. In the beginning we lack not life only, but form. Not form only, but spirit. We are blended in the one great featureless indistinguishable mass. Then a time came when the mass evolved life. And now life in its turn has evolved death. For not nature only but man's being has its seasons, its sequence of spring and autumn, summer and winter. If some one is tired and has gone to lie down, we do not pursue him with shouting and bawling. She whom I have lost has lain down to sleep for a while in the Great Inner Room. To break in upon her rest with the noise of lamentation would but show that I knew nothing of nature's Sovereign Law. That is why I ceased to mourn." CHUANG TZU

Most people do not want to think about death. Indeed it does seem a morbid topic, yet we must deal with it. We are wise to make spiritual preparation for what is inevitable and may come at any moment. Chuang Tzu's attitude toward death is unusual. This great Taoist did not follow the Confucian practice of mourning for the deceased for three years. He realized that birth and death are but two parts of the same cycle and that to share in the one is to share in the other. When death claims a loved one, we cannot but mourn, and it is good to give expression to our deep sorrow. But to carry on excessively or to prolong it without reason is folly. As the mystic says, the deceased "has lain down to sleep . . . in the Great Inner Room." To be "blended in the one great featureless indistinguishable mass" is not too happy an expression, but it means that the soul has returned to God. In God is peace.

Perhaps Chuang Tzu went to an extreme, but we would do well to reconsider some of our funeral customs.

GOD OF LIFE, take away from us the fear of death. Give us faith that in death, as in life, to be in God is to share God's infinite bliss. Amen.

53 THIS IS LIFE ETERNAL

CONFUCIANISM

Till you know about the living, how are you to know about the dead? . . . Till you have learnt to serve man, how can you serve ghosts?   ANALECTS 11.11

Tzu-lu wanted to be instructed in the appropriate rites of reverence for the dead. Then he asked whether the dead were conscious and knew each other in heaven—or its equivalent in Oriental thought. In reply, Confucius turned his disciple's thoughts toward the problem of living. There are many things about death that we cannot know now. It is more wholesome and fruitful to study how to improve man's spirit and conduct here and now. As Whittier put it:

> I know not what the future hath
> Of marvel or surprise,

Assured alone that life and death,
   His mercy underlies;
I know not where his islands lift
   Their fronded palms in air;
I only know I cannot drift
   Beyond his love and care.

By paying too much attention to the heroic past, we may be just as guilty of undue ancestor worship as were some of the ancient Chinese.

GOD GIVE US FAITH in the future, that we may serve man's deepest needs in the present. May our daily thoughts prove wholesome in the light of eternity. Amen.

54 CONTEMPT FOR LIFE

CONFUCIANISM

I like life indeed, but there is that which I like more than life, and therefore I will not seek to possess it by any improper ways. I dislike death indeed, but there is that which I dislike more than death, and therefore there are occasions when I will not avoid danger.
MENCIUS 6

"It is a most earnest thing to be alive in this world," wrote Carlyle; "to die is not sport for a man. Man's life never was a sport to him; it was a stern reality, altogether a serious matter to be alive!" Nevertheless a man's integrity is worth more than his life. "Were there as many devils in Worms as there are roof-tiles, I would go on," said Luther as he rode to his trial and was met by friends who reminded him that John Huss had been martyred under similar circumstances. Humbly he defended his integrity, concluding, "Here I stand; I cannot do otherwise—God help me!" Such heroism is too often lacking. "Truth is heavy, therefore few care to carry it."

Few choose to be martyrs. Yet when the occasion arises, some prove worthy in the conviction that man's integrity is worth more than mere survival.

GOD OF THE MARTYRS, give us faith in the spiritual calling of man. May we perceive true values amid the perils of modern life. Amen.

55 THE RETURN TO ONE'S ROOTS

TAOISM

> All things work together:
> I have watched them reverting,
> And have seen how they flourish
> And return again, each to its roots.
>
> This, I say, is the stillness:
> A retreat to one's roots;
> Or better yet, return
> To the will of God. . . .

TAO TÊ CHING 16

Lao Tzu is here saying that there is a harmony at the heart of being, could we but know it. The mystic perceives it because he has found the stillness where life's roots are grounded. The retreat to one's roots is the path to joy and peace and strength. Nor need one wait till death to taste this herb of eternity. These may seem empty words and fancies, but the mystic walks in the useful Way of love, and truth, and justice. In this Way is the will of God. It is the Way of relaxed confidence in life, of dedication to all that we know to be good. Knowledge of God brings courage, patience, and an understanding heart. It may indeed be true, as Whittier insisted, that the world's

> . . . mystics sang aright
> Of the One Life pervading all,—
> One Being's tidal rise and fall
> In soul and form, in sound and sight,—
> Eternal outflow and recall.
>
> . . . .
>
> What doth that holy Guide require?—
> No rite of pain, nor gift of blood,
> But man a kindly brotherhood,
> Looking, where duty is desire,
> To him, the beautiful and good.

The mystics had a message for this day with its tensions and fears. Truly they knew the peace of God's indwelling.

O THOU GREAT PRESENCE, may we know that peace that passes understanding through quiet sharing of the ways of truth and love. Amen.

56 ETERNAL THOUGHTS

BUDDHISM

Vigilance is the abode of eternal life, thoughtlessness is the abode of death. Those who are vigilant (who are given to reflection) do not die. The thoughtless are as if dead already.

DHAMMAPADA 21

The characteristic feature of human nature is thoughtfulness, evaluation, planning, and execution of reasoned plans.

63

If a human being chooses to live a life motivated by impulse and passion, he lives on the animal plane. The human part of him is dead even while his body is much alive. If he chooses the way of thoughtfulness ("wakefulness" is the translation of Professor Bhagwat), he lives on the plane of the divine. He is pursuing the path that leads to God, to immortality—or to Nirvana, in Buddhist terminology. The virtuous life would be impossible without thoughtfulness. The thoughtful person is the virtuous person. Good will and free, spontaneous effort to perform the thoughtful deed of kindness—this is the path to peace of mind and eternal life.

The cultivation of vigilance, or the thoughtfulness of good will, may indeed be the path that leads to eternal life.

O THOU GREAT VIVIFYING SPIRIT, may we be fully alive in mind and conscience as we live these privileged years of association with thee and our fellow men. May our thoughtfulness be energized by good will and our happiness be found through our usefulness. Amen.

57 IMMORTALITY

TAOISM

> But when you know
> What eternally is so,
> You have stature
> And stature means righteousness
> And righteousness is kingly
> And kingliness divine
> And divinity is the Way
> Which is final.

Then, though you die,
You shall not perish.

TAO TÊ CHING 16

Lao Tzu, legendary author of the Tao Tê Ching, here suggests that when one identifies himself with truth and all reality, he necessarily becomes good and follows in the Way that is everlasting. "Then, though you die, you shall not perish." Immortality is a quality which is experienced even in this life. In our effort to explain our hopes of immortality, logic fails; the poetry of faith becomes our best servant.

> Strong Son of God, immortal Love,
>   Whom we, that have not seen thy face,
>   By faith, and faith alone, embrace,
> Believing where we cannot prove;
>
> Thine are these orbs of light and shade;
>   Thou madest Life in man and brute;
>   Thou madest Death; and lo, thy foot
> Is on the skull which thou hast made.
>
> Thou wilt not leave us in the dust;
>   Thou madest man, he knows not why;
>   He thinks he was not made to die;
> And thou hast made him: thou art just.

Anyone who thinks deeply will agree that "now we see through a glass darkly"—that is, we fail to visualize immortal existence. This is an area for faith and hope.

LORD OF LIFE, may our daily desires be consistent with our hope of immortality and with a belief in the eternal value of the human soul. Amen.

For God created man for incorruption,
and made him in the image of his own eternity,
but through the devil's envy death entered the world,
and those who belong to his party experience it.
But the souls of the righteous are in the hand of God,
and no torment will ever touch them.
In the eyes of the foolish they seemed to have died,
and their departure was thought to be an affliction,
and their going from us to be their destruction;
but they are at peace.
For though in the sight of men they were punished,
their hope is full of immortality.
Having been disciplined a little, they will receive great good,
because God tested them and found them worthy of himself. . . .
They will govern nations and rule over peoples,
and the Lord will reign over them for ever.
Those who trust in him will understand truth,
and the faithful will abide with him in love. . . .

WISDOM OF SOLOMON 2:23-3:9

This beautiful passage from the Jewish Apocrypha conceives of man as the image of eternity, who only through wickedness experiences death. He has the dreadful freedom to neglect true being and to let himself be pushed around by passions, desires, appetites, and ignorance. When he finds himself—that is, his real spiritual integrity—he wins immortality and shares the being of truth and love and righteousness. The writer of this scripture does not explain what is meant by immortality, except to say that the souls of the righteous are in God's being and are at peace. Little do we know about the mysteries of eternity. Certainly man's being is far more than the simple consciousness of the organism. God's consciousness is not that of an organism, and man shares God's being.

The righteous eternally share God's rule of the world in that, like God, they are creative and just, and their judgments on human conduct ultimately prevail.

Eternal God, as we are tried, may we be found worthy of the divine fellowship, now and forever. May we daily renew our faith in the immortal value of every soul and in the bliss of thy presence. Amen.

59 THE SOUL'S SALVATION

BUDDHISM

Enough, Ananda! Do not let yourself be troubled; do not weep! Have I not already, on former occasions, told you that it is in the nature of all things most near and dear unto us that we must divide ourselves from them, leave them, sever ourselves from them? How then, Ananda, can this be possible—whereas anything whatever born, brought into being, and organized, contains within itself the inherent necessity of dissolution—how then can this be possible, that such a being should not be dissolved? No such condition can exist! For a long time, Ananda, have you been very near to me by acts of love, kind and good, that never varies, and is beyond all measure. . . . You have done well, Ananda! Be earnest in effort, and you too shall soon be free from the great evils . . . from sensuality, from individuality, from delusion, and from ignorance!

. . . .

Decay is inherent in all component things! Work out your salvation with diligence. MAHA-PARINIBBANA-SUTTA 5.35; 6.10

These are supposed to be the words of the dying Buddha at the end of a ministry of forty-five years. It is his appraisal of the transitory nature of life. It expresses his sense of urgency of the need for salvation. Since the human organism is composed of parts, Buddha thought it inevitable that those parts, having once mysteriously come together, must mysteriously also dissolve. This spiritual understanding may prepare us for the inevitable whenever it comes. Salvation lies in gaining that peace which passes understanding—the peace that is eternal.

The strength of Buddhism was that it faced the inevitable with realistic candor without losing faith in the universe.

ETERNAL GOD, may we, realizing that the inevitable is neither good nor bad, have that peace of mind which survives all circumstances and leads us on to thy salvation. Amen.

60   GOAL OF THE RELIGIOUS LIFE

BUDDHISM

(Theological speculations) profit not, have not to do with the fundamentals of religion, tend not to absence of passion, quiescence, supreme wisdom, and Nirvana.   MAJJHIMA 63

Perhaps the Buddha overstated his case here. But it is clear that he regarded the experience of religion as far more important than theological speculations. There is a place for theology and philosophy. But religion is essentially a way of life, and the stress must remain on its practice. For the Buddha salvation was an experience which he called

Nirvana—the absence of passion, quiescence, supreme wisdom. It is the experience of the absolute bliss which fills him who has conquered the world, as Christian saints have conquered it. Buddha thought that it was necessary to conquer desire, thirst, craving, which keep men ever discontented. The resulting bliss is attainable now and is eternal.

There is little danger that the average person will be carried away by futile theological speculation. It is the modern temper to stress the practical aspects of the spiritual life rather than theology. Actually we need some kind of theology, but its test is in experience.

O WORD OF GOD, grant us the wisdom to put first things first, to understand and practice the way of salvation. May we live by a principle which frees us from emotional dependence upon the fortunes of life and brings abiding happiness. Amen.

61 HOW TO BE SAVED

BUDDHISM

A Bodhisattva resolves: I take upon myself the burden of all suffering. . . . My endeavors do not merely aim at my own deliverance. SIKSHASAMUCCAYA 280-81 (VAJRADHVAJA SUTRA)

Taken from a document of Mahayana Buddhism, this passage states the most characteristic attitude of the Mahayana Buddhist monk. It is the attitude of complete dedication to the salvation of the world, rather than to one's own personal salvation. One may detect an element of personal aggrandizement in the ideal of one's saving a whole universe. Yet motives are hard to assess. In any case, the

Mahayanist gained considerable maturity by rejecting the goal of personal salvation and substituting for it the ideal of living for others, which was the principle involved in the Mahayana myths. Paradoxically, the unselfish ideal led to the fuller realization of personal salvation.

There are untried ways in which we may contribute to the welfare or salvation of others without going beyond the means at our disposal. Missionary enterprise is much more enlightened than many people realize.

O FATHER OF MANKIND, may we cultivate the outward look and strive to become genuinely interested in the happiness of others. May we be willing to share the burdens of all peoples as our ability permits. Amen.

62 GOD WITHIN

JAINISM

Man! Thou art thine own friend; why wishest thou for a friend beyond thyself? Whom he knows as a dweller on high, him he should know as a dweller far (from sin); and whom he knows as a dweller far (from sin), him he should know as a dweller on high. AKARANGA SUTRA 1.3, 3.4

Here is a radical humanism expressed by Mahavira, founder of Jainism. He is trying to say that the Hindu God, Brahman, is too philosophically remote to have any real value to a human being. Brahman cannot help a man as much as a man can help himself; man is his own best friend in this perplexing and frustrating universe. The "dweller on high" (God) is not Brahman, splendid and remote, but the essential God for which good men strive. It may be that Mahavira was prejudiced in his understanding of Hinduism. Certainly he was not consistent in his theology. His most valid insight was that God is in some way to be found deep in the heart of human experience. God is not space, but spirit. His essence is spiritual perfection. This is scarcely more than a hint in Mahavira, but it is at least a hint.

It may be that the inward reverence which man feels toward the good is a valid clue to God's spiritual reality.

COMPASSIONATE GOD, may we perceive the good in human experience and find thee suddenly warming our hearts and inspiring our lives. Amen.

63 THE IMPORTANT THING

SIKHISM

Nanak very humbly undertakes expression,
Saying self-denial is of slight avail;
To please thee is man's best aspiration,
O thou who art eternal, dwelling ever in repose. . . .
Pilgrimage and penance and free-will giving
Gain for one no slight grain of merit,
Unless one hearken and his heart be loving,
Cleansed within by a meditative bath.

GRANTH

Nanak's was a religion of the spirit. He perceived the essential superstition and idolatry of symbols, ritual, and pilgrimage when regarded as ends in themselves or as magical devices for gaining merit. We should note that he did not flatly condemn pilgrimage and ritual, for he used the word "unless." The important part of the experience of salvation is our mystic sensitivity to the spirit of God, our love to all men, the purity of our motives, and the clarity of our thought or meditation. These are the experiences which bring peace of heart and human harmony and lead to the spirit's salvation.

The motive is the important thing, of course, in any human action, whether it be pilgrimage, almsgiving, punishment, or pleasure.

FATHER OF TRUTH, cleanse us from unconscious superstitions and magical preconceptions in our own behavior and make us thoughtful, kind, and pure. Amen.

64 THE SPIRIT OF SERVICE

TAOISM

> *Quicken them, feed them;*
> *Quicken but do not possess them.*
> *Act and be independent;*
> *Be the chief but never the lord;*
> *This describes the mystic virtue.*
>
> TAO TÊ CHING 10

For most of our favors to our fellow men we expect favors in return. In fact, we often perform acts of kindness to one from whom we are seeking greater favors than we give. There is a legitimate place in life for an exchange of gifts in harmony with the golden rule. But the noblest service is free and completely benevolent, as suggested by most of the great religions. Jesus said, "I was hungry and you gave me food." The Teacher of Righteousness at Qumran expressed the same feeling (in the Dead Sea Scrolls). Selfless service is what Lao Tzu was urging in the scripture quoted above. Thomas Curtis Clarke has caught that spirit in his poem:

> I sought his love in sun and stars,
>   And where the wild seas roll,
> And found it not. As mute I stood,
>   Fear overwhelmed my soul;
> But when I gave to one in need,
> I found the Lord of Love indeed.

There is, of course, a limit to how far one can go in rendering benevolent service, depending on our resources. But few of us ever approach that limit.

MERCIFUL GOD, make us to be merciful that we, like thee, may give with no thought of selfish gain. Amen.

65 THE EVERLASTING WORD

STOICISM

O Zeus, most honored of immortals, known by many names,
Ever omnipotent, nature's lord, ruling all by law:
    We call to thee.
For it is right that mortal men should seek thee.
As thine own children we alone enjoy thy gift of speech and
    symbol—
All we who for a while inhabit this broad earth.
So shall I always sing to thee, and praise thy power for ever.
Truly this one great universe, revolving round the earth,
Fulfills thy will, easily controlled by thee.
Thou hast in thy strong hand the useful, two-edged, fiery, ever-
    breathing

73

Thunderbolt, under whose blows all nature's works are done.
Thou art the source of universal mind which penetrates all
   things,
Showing thy radiance as it orders elements both great and small.
Truly thou art the absolute and glorious ruler of all things.
No earthly thing occurs, O God, apart from thee:
Not in the highest heaven, nor deepest sea—except
      What wicked men in ignorance do!
Thou canst instruct the wise, bring order out of chaos.
Through thee the loveless can be made adorable.
For in one whole thou hast combined the evil with the total good,
So to enhance the everlasting word, essence of all things.
Poor mortal men of evil heart, missing this noble truth
      Though ever wishing for the good,
Discern not nor obey God's universal law,
Which if perceived with understanding heart would bless with
   noble life.

  .   .   .   .

Bountiful Zeus, veiled in deep mystery, thunder's lord,
Keep us from sorry ignorance.
Banish it, father, from our lives, and grant
That we may share the truth by which thou guidest all things.
Thus we, being honored, may thee honor too, praising thy works
   forever,
      As seemeth good for mortal men.
No greater bliss may men or gods enjoy
Than evermore to chant the hymns of universal law.

                                        HYMN OF CLEANTHES

   These words of Cleanthes, a great Stoic of the third century B.C., express what many have sought to say in other
faiths. In the tradition of Greek religious drama and philosophy, Cleanthes saw God as one supreme ruler of the universe, whose essence is reason, law, spirit. This reminds us
of John 1:1, "In the beginning was the Word (Logos,
Reason), and the Word was with God, and the Word was
God." Reason (or wisdom) can become very much alive in
dedicated temples of the human body.

Unfortunately, for many of us, reason is a mere tool for devising ways of getting what we want, not a clue to God's reality.

GOD GRANT that we may at all times think clearly and bring our actions into harmony with the spiritual laws of the heavenly king, the father of our spirits. Amen.

66 MOTIVATION OF THE SPIRIT

HINDUISM

Quickly I come
To those who offer me
Every action,
Worship me only,
Their dearest delight,
With devotion undaunted.

Because they love me
These are my bondsmen
And I shall save them
From mortal sorrow
And all the waves
Of life's deathly ocean.

Be absorbed in me,
Lodge your mind in me:
Thus you shall dwell in me,
Do not doubt it,
Here and hereafter.

BHAGAVAD-GITA 12, 6-8

Passages like this from the Bhagavad-Gita help to explain why Gandhi found solace and inspiration in reading it. Krishna, God's incarnate son or avatar, is here speaking to his human friend Arjuna. Through Krishna God enters intimately into the life of man. God is not far away; he is ready to commune with us when we need him. The only thing that keeps him away is our failure to seek and to love him. He does not force himself on us. Our union with him gives us immortality. Thus Hindus read in their "Song of the Beloved."

As in other scriptures, here are promises which sometimes seem unfulfilled, since mortal sorrow is bound to come to all. However, salvation does not consist in freedom from trouble, but in moral victory over those troubles.

SPIRIT OF GOD, may our dearest delight be communion with thy invisible Presence whom we can know to be all good and all loving. Amen.

67 THE MYSTIC UNITY

TAOISM

> *Stop your senses,*
> *Close the doors;*
> *Let sharp things be blunted,*
> *Tangles resolved,*
> *The light tempered*
> *And turmoil subdued;*
> *For this is the mystic unity. . . .*
>
> TAO TÊ CHING 56

There are times when we can find God in the crowded street or in the opportunities to serve in office or byway. But many people miss seeing him "in haunts of wretchedness and need" because they have not taken time to look for him in quietness first. God eludes our search, not because he does not want us to find him, but because of our naïve notions of his nature and habitat. As Emerson wrote:

> Thou metest him by centuries,
> And lo! he passes like the breeze;
> Thou seek'st in glade and galaxy,
> He hides in pure transparency;
> Thou askest in fountains and in fires,
> He is the essence that inquires.

Some of us may need to be shocked out of complacency with our religious experience in order that we may broaden and deepen it.

O GOD, may we not miss the vision of the mystic unity because of our concern with details of sense and the turmoil of life. May our service to man be inspired by the sense of thy holiness. Amen.

68   PURITY AND POWER

SHINTO

Brush away all the stains from the heart, then divine power will pour into it.
      MIKI, founder of Tenri Kyo—a faith-healing sect of Japan
To be of one heart with the Great Divinity is to live fully and forever.   KUROZUMI, founder of another peasant sect

These founders of sectarian Shinto realized that purity of heart is required for the fullest effectiveness in living. They shared the insight of Tennyson, whose Sir Galahad asserted:

My strength is as the strength of ten,
Because my heart is pure.

. . . .

So keep I fair thro' faith and prayer
A virgin heart in work and will.

Our modern age has put so much faith in science that we now fear that the stress should have been upon the heart. Technology is rising up against us. We need technology, but it must be our servant, not our master. The pure heart in interpersonal and international affairs is far more important than technology. It alone can give us real power and save us from destruction. The world's present struggle is more spiritual than material.

Knowledge comes, but wisdom lingers, and I linger on the shore,
And the individual withers, and the world is more and more.

As we see God's purpose revealed in increasing international interdependence and the evident necessity of universal good will, we must do what we can to increase purity of heart and understanding among men.

O GOD, may we fear, not simple piety, but godless ambition in ourselves and neighbors. May we put our faith in the universal love that is divine. Amen.

Arise! Awake! Approach the great and learn. Like the sharp edge of a razor is that path, so the wise say—hard to tread and difficult to cross. KATHA UPANISHAD 1.3.14

In this passage from the Katha Upanishad, Nachiketa is being advised to persist in his effort to learn the truth about immortality and God. It is as difficult as crossing the razor's edge—an analogy comparable with the New Testament figure of going through the eye of a needle. But the goal is of inestimable worth and should never be abandoned. Fortunate are we if we can learn from great men, either personally or through their writings.

Considering how difficult is truth, it is no wonder that the great thinkers differ. To learn from them means, not to accept their conclusions, but to emulate their earnest quest for the eternal.

O GOD OF THE LIVING, make us so alive and awake to our spiritual natures that we shall continually seek to understand life and its values. May we not be discouraged. Amen.

Om! Verily, the dawn is the head of the sacrificial horse; the sun, his eye; the wind, his breath; universal fire, his open mouth. The year is the body of the sacrificial horse; the sky, his back; the atmosphere, his belly; the earth, the underpart of his belly; the quarters, his flanks . . . the seasons, his limbs . . . the stars, his bones; the clouds, his flesh.

BRIHADARANYAKA UPANISHAD 1.1.1

The horse sacrifice was the most elaborate of the sacrifices of ancient India. It was costly and cruel. Spiritual-minded Hindus allegorized it and did away with the necessity of sacrifice, as suggested in this quotation from the Brihadaranyaka Upanishad. This classic was written no later than the seventh century B.C. It pioneered in the trend toward less ritual and more spiritual insight.

It is no easy task to bring about a simplification of ritual, although spiritual growth requires it. Ritual can become burdensome and uninspiring. We need a ritual that is relevant today, one that will express moral motivation on a world-wide scale.

GOD OF BEAUTY, give us the imagination to create symbols of truth and beauty that shall serve our generation in its deepest needs. Amen.

Verily, a person is a sacrifice. His (first) twenty-four years are the morning libation. . . . When a man hungers, thirsts, and abstains from pleasures, that is the initiatory rite. When one eats and drinks and enjoys himself—then he joins in the . . . ceremonies. . . . Austerity, almsgiving, uprightness, harmlessness, truthfulness—these are one's gifts for the priests. . . . Death is the ablution after the ceremony.

CHANDOGYA UPANISHAD 3.16-17, *passim*

This passage imaginatively translates old ritual in terms of living. Not quoted above is one section which states that laughter and feasting and conjugal love are the chant and recitation of the ritual of life itself. The whole passage makes all of life as meaningful as the ritual had been thought to be and every bit as sacred. The Hindu scriptures offer a magnificent challenge for man to regard life—his own and that of all others—as a sacred trust.

The real purpose of ritual is to remind us of the true values of life itself. If it fails in this and becomes its own end, we are to blame.

CREATOR OF ALL LIFE, help us to discern true human values and to dedicate ourselves to their enlargement through our worship of thee. Amen.

"I torture not my body with penances" (*to do so would be to torment God*). *"I lame not my feet in pilgrimage to holy places"* (*since my body is God's temple*). *"I spend not my time in reading the Vedas"* (*from which I get the religious experience of others while neglecting my own*). *"But I strive to attain Thy two Sacred Feet"* (*thus to do God's will as if my own*).   TO SHAKTI

These quotations are from a Hymn of Mahakalarudra to Mahakali (Shakti), with comments by Avalon, alias Woodroffe, in the latter's book entitled *Shakti*. The Mother Goddess, in some form, was universally worshiped in the childhood of the race. In India the Mother Goddess was known as Kali or Durga or Shakti. It might be thought that the worship of Shakti, symbol of female energy, would not result in such enlightened consecration as is here expressed. But Shakti became a symbol of the universal force which expresses universal love and care. Reverence for motherhood reflects this insight today.

The fatherhood of God is symbolic of God's creative care. His motherhood is just as pregnant with spiritual insight. Both symbols, and all others, are meant to bring God into our lives.

GOD GIVE US prophetic insight and the power to perceive divinity in common places. May we distinguish between that which has genuine religious value and that which merely survives through custom. Amen.

Even if he recites a large number of scriptural texts but, being slothful, does not act accordingly, he is like a cowherd counting the cows of others, he has no share in religious life. Even if he recites only a small number, if he is one who acts rightly in accordance with the law, he, having forsaken passion, hatred, and folly, being possessed of true knowledge and serenity of mind, being free from worldly desires both in this world and the next, has a share in the religious life.   DHAMMAPADA 19-20

Writes Radhakrishnan, "The Buddha's teaching is a way of life, not a way of talking. We are what we love and care for." It is quite possible to substitute glowing thoughts and memorized verses for right acts and genuine good will. The Buddha opposed useless speculation in theology and metaphysics, preferring to cultivate good will and right conduct. Thoughtfulness is good; meditation and self-control are good; but action must follow reflection and good intentions. Action perfects the good life.

Not all sacred scripture is of equal value. It takes a discerning spirit to select such portions of holy writ as will inspire and satisfy our lives.

O GOD, may our experience of religion be such that the commonplace shall become holy, and the holy shall create a brotherhood of service. Amen.

Not by matted hair, not by lineage, not by caste does one become a Brahmin. He is a Brahmin in whom there are truth and righteousness. He is blessed.

What is the use of matted hair, O fool, what of the raiment of goatskins? Thine inward nature is full of wickedness; the outside thou makest clean. DHAMMAPADA 393-394

In India, matted hair and the wearing of animal skins were supposed to indicate special holiness. Every culture has its symbolic forms. But in India as elsewhere there were prophets who perceived that the modes of outward behavior were far less important than the cleansing of the soul through wisdom and good motives. It is just as simple as that. Holiness is absolutely conditioned by good will and enlightenment. There is no substitute for purification of the heart. As Jesus said, cleansing the outside of the cup is less important than cleansing the inside (Luke 11:39). One may even become so self-satisfied with the observance of external forms of righteousness that such observance will stand in the way of real goodness.

No deception is more damaging than self-deception in the quest of righteousness.

O GOD, create in us a clean heart and renew a right spirit within us. Amen.

The Master said, High office filled by men of narrow views, ritual performed without reverence, the forms of mourning observed without grief—these are things I cannot bear to see!

ANALECTS 3.26

When substance overbalances refinement, crudeness results. When refinement overbalances substance, there is superficiality. When refinement and substance are balanced one has Great Man.

ANALECTS 6.16

"Honor both spirit and form, both sentiment within and symbol without," urged Ramakrishna. This theme has been expressed by the prophets of all traditions. Sincere good will needs to be conveyed by means of outward courtesy. Either without the other leaves half a man. "Sacrifice is not a thing coming to a man from without; it issues from within him, and has its birth in his heart. When the heart is deeply moved, expression is given to it by ceremonies; and hence, only men of ability and virtue can give complete exhibition to the idea of sacrifice."

Individually and internationally, real respect and courtesy will go a long way toward achieving a peaceful world.

GOD OF PEACE, make our hearts sincere that we may be instruments of thy peace and kindness through common acts of courtesy and respect. Amen.

A fool brings grief on himself with the thought: "This son is mine, this wealth is mine." How can he, if he does not even belong to himself, be the possessor of a son or wealth?

DHAMMAPADA 62

Ownership is a relative term. The thought in this passage is not to deny possessive ownership of a relative sort, but rather to deny absolute ownership. Considering the brevity of human life, nothing can belong to us in any ultimate sense except character. Yet we tend to be confident of our ownership of material goods, wife or husband, and children. Material goods really belong to the universe—they are divine property. Our use of them is a privilege, not a right, and as a privilege we ought to share them with others so far as that is possible. In a profounder sense our children do not belong to us. Not even do we possess ourselves. Our lives and our children are entrusted to us, with the obligation to cultivate the fullest possible expression of spiritual personality. We do great harm to our children when we try to possess them, that is, to make them express our personalities rather than help them to express their own.

By being too "possessive" of goods or family and friends, we may stand in the way of our own deepest and most abiding happiness.

MAKER AND OWNER of the spheres, may we regard all that we own as but a brief loan from thee to be used for the perfection of the spirit. Amen.

The crooked shall be made straight
And the rough places plain;
The pools shall be filled
And the worn renewed;
The needy shall receive
And the rich shall be perplexed.

So the Wise Man cherishes the One,
As a standard to the world:
Not displaying himself,
He is famous;
Not asserting himself, he is distinguished;
Not boasting his powers,
He is effective;
Taking no pride in himself,
He is chief.

Because he is no competitor,
No one in all the world
Can compete with him.

TAO TÊ CHING 22

The first stanza above expresses faith in the justice of
the divine Way. It reminds us of the prophet Isaiah:

Every valley shall be lifted up,
    and every mountain and hill be made low;
the uneven ground shall become level,
    and the rough places plain.   (40:4)

Justice cannot but result from the life that is at one with the divine will, that conforms with the Way, that "cherishes the One as a standard to the world." Unsought fame, humble leadership, and achievement come to him whose only aim is to make the Way real in his life. Justice shall flow from him as water from a springing fountain. Blessed shall be the fruit of his spirit.

The good man fears no competition. What could be happier than that all should compete as benefactors of justice!

O GOD, may the foundations of our lives be such that we can never be overcome by the fortunes of life. Amen.

78 THE PLANNED LIFE

CONFUCIANISM

In all things success depends on previous preparation, and without such previous preparation there is sure to be failure. . . . If principles of conduct have been previously determined, the practice of them will be inexhaustible. DOCTRINE OF THE MEAN

The Confucian ideal of planned action may seem far removed from the Taoist principle of inaction suggested by previous meditations. Yet even Taoism proposes certain principles of effortless achievement, in a background of humility and integrity. Both religions demand wisdom in meeting life's problems. In truth, unless one first determines the principles on which his life shall be planned, his actions will be likely to nullify each other. Effective living requires the meditative approach, with commitment to the good principles arising from such reflection.

Wisdom demands not only that life shall be planned but

also that the plans shall be revised from time to time in view of new insights.

SPIRIT OF GOD, may we be not like the beasts, living by impulse, but like sons of God, living by ideals and virtuous plans. Amen.

79 THOUGHT, WORD, AND DEED

ZOROASTRIANISM

A Mazda-worshiper am I, of Zarathustra's order; so do I confess as a praiser and confessor, and I therefore praise aloud the well-thought thought, the word well spoken, and the deed well done. YASNA 12

Zoroaster conceived of Mazda as the one and only God, the God of light. To him this meant the God of enlightenment, truth, civilization, and righteousness. Zoroaster's was a practical religion, calling for a well-balanced combination of thought, word, and deed in a life of peace and good will. Certainly the thoughtful life needs to be cultivated as the basis of all else that is good. As Mencius said, "There are the footpaths along the hills;—if suddenly they be used, they become roads; and if as suddenly they are not used, the wild grass fills them up. Now, the wild grass fills up your mind." Wisdom is promoted by persistent inquiry. "He who likes to put questions becomes enlarged; he who uses only his own views becomes smaller than he was." Words should be used with discrimination and care. "Words which are simple, while their meaning is far-reaching, are good words." "Open not thy mouth to speak evil."

The real test of thoughts and words is deeds. "Show me

your faith apart from your works, and I by my works will
show you my faith."

GREAT TEACHER, grant us the patience necessary for the
cultivation of the intellectual life. May we not disdain the
prosaic exercises of logical thinking and word analysis in
our effort to reach the truth of God and to understand
our fellow man. Amen.

80 PIETY FOR LIFE'S SAKE

ISLAM

There is no piety in turning your faces toward the east or the
west, but he is pious who believeth in God and the last day and
the angels and the scriptures and the prophets; who for the love
of God disburseth his wealth to his kindred, and to the orphans,
and the needy, and the wayfarer, and those who ask, and for
ransoming; who observeth prayer, and payeth the legal alms, and
who is one of those who are faithful to their engagements when
they have engaged in them, and patient under ills and hardships
and in time of trouble. . . .   KORAN 2:172

It is almsgiving if you make adjustment between a couple; and
if you help a man in the matter of his riding-animal and mount
him upon her or lift his baggage for him upon her. A good word
is almsgiving . . . and it is almsgiving when you ward danger off
the road.   TRADITIONS

Both the Koran and the later scripture of Islam here cited
identify devotion to God with deeds of kindness to those in
need. The good word, faithfulness in promises, patience
in hardships, gallantry in emergencies on the highway,
generosity in family relationships—these are the real tests
of godliness. It is important that we pray, but it is not im-

portant that we kneel, sit, or stand, or that we face a customary way; nor is it important that we pray in English
or in Hebrew or in spoken words at all. In the spirit of
these passages, one might even omit belief in certain out-
grown cosmologies. Surely the greater part of goodness lies
in the field of human relations.

Jesus once said, "You tithe mint and dill and cummin,
and have neglected the weightier matters of the law, justice
and mercy and faith; these you ought to have done, without
neglecting the others." His followers will measure godliness
entirely in terms of love and service.

O God, may we feel thy nearness in the service of human
need and in the courteous word. Amen.

81　THE GOOD LIFE

OLD TESTAMENT

*"For this commandment which I command you this day is not
too hard for you, neither is it far off. It is not in heaven, that you
should say, 'Who will go up for us to heaven, and bring it to us,
that we may hear it and do it?' Neither is it beyond the sea,
that you should say, 'Who will go over the sea for us, and bring
it to us, that we may hear it and do it?' But the word is very
near you; it is in your mouth and in your heart, so that you can
do it.*

*"See, I have set before you this day life and good, death and
evil."*   DEUTERONOMY 30:11-15

The difficult, far-off aspirations may so absorb our minds
that we miss seeing the simple path of duty close at hand.
Moses offered Israel the choice between self-indulgent

heathenism and self-restraining law. The laws which he offered were practical for the aims of the best possible society for those times. Like choices always confront man. Writes Radhakrishnan, "Great spiritual issues are at stake today. Intellectually and morally our world walks on the edge of an abyss. If a democracy is educated, and has imaginative vision and moral courage, it can bring about a social revolution without violence. The democratic way of life is not a law of nature. It is not an evolutionary process destined to establish itself, wherever human beings value their manhood. It is a precious possession won by enlightened people after ages of struggle, and can be lost in a dark age, when men grow indifferent to it. It is an idea, not a system, and we must guard it with the utmost care, especially at a time when the speeding up of a mechanical civilization is engendering mass subservience. Democratic methods of reform can cope with revolutionary situations. Any economic system which disregards the personality of the worker, or for the profits of the few exposes him to soul-destroying want or corrupting idleness, must be ended."

Our leaders are providing us with ample insights into the human predicament today. What we need is the courage of decision.

God GIVE US perceptive hearts, courage to act, and persistence to believe in the reality of present dangers and opportunities. May we choose life and good rather than death and evil. Amen.

Do not push forward a wagon;—
You will only raise the dust about yourself.
Do not think of all your anxieties;—
You will only make yourself ill.

SHIH CHING

Pushing forward a wagon is a figure suggesting impatience with getting a job done. One who behaves in such a way cannot wait to get in front of the wagon; he pushes from behind. But does the wagon get there any sooner than if he took time to pull it from in front? Meanwhile he will breathe the dust of impatience. The point of the quatrain is that worry does not pay. If you have anxieties, it is folly to fret about them. Cool analysis of their basis and patient forming of plans for improvement—this would be wisdom. To be without anxiety does not mean to be lazy. Even Jesus did not mean that when he told his disciples to "consider the lilies of the field." In discussing this situation Kierkegaard wrote, "When a sailor lies in his boat and leaves everything to chance in the storm, and does not know anything at all to do, then we do not speak of him as a perfect sailor. But if the brave seaman knows how to steer, if with skill and energy and persistence he combats the wind and storm, works himself out of danger, then we admire him. If late in the forenoon we see a man who has arisen late, sluggish and yet hungry, waiting to get his food by chance, then we do not commend him; but if early in the morning we see the active worker, or even if we do not see him, see that he has already been there, that the fisherman has already been out with his net, that the herdsman has already put away his churn, then we commend the fisher-man and the herdsman. To work is the perfection of the human."

No human situation justifies worry. It may call for care-ful study, but anxiety is not conducive to problem-solving.

GOD OF PEACE, may we possess our souls at all times de-spite the frustrations of life. May we find our peace in a sane combination of faith and effort. Amen.

83 TREASURES IN HEAVEN

NEW TESTAMENT

Do not lay up for yourselves treasures on earth, where moth and rust consume and where thieves break in and steal, but lay up for yourselves treasures in heaven, where neither moth nor rust consumes and where thieves do not break in and steal. For where your treasure is, there will your heart be also.

. . . .

Therefore I tell you, do not be anxious about your life, what you shall eat or what you shall drink, nor about your body, what you shall put on. Is not life more than food, and the body more than clothing? Look at the birds of the air: they neither sow nor reap nor gather into barns, and yet your heavenly Father feeds them. Are you not of more value than they? And which of you by being anxious can add one cubit to his span of life? And why are you anxious about clothing? Consider the lilies of the field, how they grow; they neither toil nor spin; yet I tell you, even Solomon in all his glory was not arrayed like one of these. But if God so clothes the grass of the field, which today is alive and tomorrow is thrown into the oven, will he not much more clothe you, O men of little faith? Therefore do not be anxious, saying, "What shall we eat?" or "What shall we drink?" or "What shall we wear?" For the Gentiles seek all these things; and your heavenly

Father knows that you need them all. But seek first his kingdom and his righteousness, and all these things shall be yours as well.

Therefore do not be anxious about tomorrow, for tomorrow will be anxious for itself. Let the day's own troubles be sufficient for the day.   MATTHEW 6:19-21, 25-34

Men are worth more than birds or flowers but not because of their fine clothes or their rich food. It is by realizing our true natures, fashioned in God's image, that we human beings surpass the birds and the flowers. Wrote Kierkegaard, "God created man in his own image; ought it not to be glorious to be thus clad! The Gospel says, in order to praise the lily, that it surpasses Solomon in glory—ought it not to be infinitely more glorious to resemble God! . . . Since God is invisible, no one can *visibly* resemble him. That is exactly why the lily does not resemble God—because the glory of the lily is the visible."

The clothing of God's love and righteousness is glorious beyond comparison and will never wear out.

GOD HELP US to find our joy in the eternal values of the divine image, in love, service, and wisdom. Amen.

84 THE SOURCE OF HAPPINESS

CONFUCIANISM

Those who externally attach great importance to material things are always inwardly anxious. Those who act without regard for moral principles are always externally in a dangerous position. And such persons are always inwardly afraid. . . . When a man's mind is peaceful and happy, then sights below the ordinary will satisfy the eye; even sounds below the ordinary will content the ear; coarse rice, vegetables, and soup will be enough for the mouth; clothing of coarse cloth and sandals made from rough cords will give comfort to the body. . . . This may indeed be called . . . making material things one's servant. HSUN-TZU

The Confucian Hsun-tzu was no doubt inspired by his master who centuries earlier had said, "To eat only vegetables without meat, to drink only water, to have only one's bent arm as a pillow: there can be joy in such a life. But to become rich and honored through injustices: for me such joy may be compared to an evanescent cloud." Rich food and fine clothing are bad only if they distract the spirit of man from its true fulfillment in thoughtfulness, truth, love, and beauty. Ambition and vanity sometimes trick us into believing that happiness can be bought and preserved indefinitely.

There is no mechanical way of measuring our success in the spiritual life, wherein the goal is not getting but serving. The intuitive insight of those who are spiritual is the only measure we have.

GOD OF GRACE, give us the grace to understand true values. Take from our souls all vanity and help us to treasure the riches of humility, love, and truth. Amen.

85 CONTENTMENT

NEW TESTAMENT

Blessed are the poor in spirit, for theirs is the kingdom of heaven.

Blessed are those who mourn, for they shall be comforted.

Blessed are the meek, for they shall inherit the earth.

Blessed are those who hunger and thirst for righteousness, for they shall be satisfied.

Blessed are the merciful, for they shall obtain mercy.

Blessed are the pure in heart, for they shall see God.

Blessed are the peacemakers, for they shall be called sons of God.

Blessed are those who are persecuted for righteousness' sake, for theirs is the kingdom of heaven.

Blessed are you when men shall revile you and persecute you and utter all kinds of evil against you falsely on my account. Rejoice and be glad, for your reward is great in heaven, for so men persecuted the prophets who were before you.

MATTHEW 5:3-11

The religious person, like everyone else, wants to be happy. The Hindu mystic seeks perfect bliss—ananda—through union with God. The Buddha sought it and found it in enlightenment and his subsequent peace of heart. The bliss of purity is blessedness. It is true contentment, peace of heart. Such experience belongs to the meek and merciful, the poor and sincere, the peacemakers and the pure in heart, those who strive for perfection and who remain steadfast in persecution, who forgive and seek to make all men their brothers. The true disciple ever gains new insights into the paths of contentment. As John Oxenham wrote:

Blessed are they that have eyes to see.
    They shall find God everywhere.
    They shall see Him where others see stones.
Blessed are they that have understanding hearts.
    To them shall be multiplied kingdoms of delight.
Blessed are they that see visions.
    They shall rejoice in the hidden ways of God.
Blessed are the song-ful of soul,
    They carry light and joy to shadowed lives.
Blessed are they who know the power of Love.
    They dwell in God for God is Love.

What a travesty upon religion to conceive of it as the sad way!

O GOD OF BLISS, may we by sharing know the bliss that passes all understanding. Deliver us from anxiety and make our hearts pure. Amen.

86 WHAT GOD REQUIRES

> *The royal court is dignified, sedate,*
> *While farmers' fields are overgrown with weeds;*
> *The granaries are empty and yet they*
> *Are clad in rich-embroidered silken gowns.*
> *They have sharp swords suspended at their sides;*
> *With glutted wealth, they gorge with food and drink.*
>
> *It is, the people say,*
> *The boastfulness of brigandage,*
> *But surely not the Way!*

TAO TÊ CHING 53

Lao Tzu, prophet of the Way, was displeased by the contrast which he noted between the luxury of the royal court and the poverty of the people. It looked to him like a case of brigandage, or gangsterism, where those in power thought themselves entitled to all they could get from the people without giving anything in return. This is not the divine Way. In truth, the display of wealth in the midst of poverty is bound to cause resentment. The just ruler will not find time for display if dutifully he seeks the cause and cure of the poverty. Whether ruler, merchant, or member of a profession, the Way requires a responsibility which leaves neither time nor desire for idleness or vanity.

The world's present poverty is a proper object of America's concern. The solution will be complex.

GOD KEEP US in the Way of the just, the Way of those who care. May we show a real concern for the complete well-being of the many. Amen.

87 UNDEFILED RELIGION

NEW TESTAMENT

If any one thinks he is religious, and does not bridle his tongue but deceives his heart, this man's religion is vain. Religion that is pure and undefiled before God and the Father is this: to visit orphans and widows in their affliction, and to keep oneself unstained from the world.

My brethren, show no partiality as you hold the faith of our Lord Jesus Christ, the Lord of glory. For if a man with gold rings and in fine clothing comes into your assembly, and a poor man in shabby clothing also comes in, and you pay attention to the one who wears the fine clothing and say, "Have a seat here, please," while you say to the poor man, "Stand there," or, "Sit at my feet," have you not made distinctions among yourselves, and become judges with evil thoughts? Listen, my beloved brethren. Has not God chosen those who are poor in the world to be rich in faith and heirs of the kingdom which he has promised to those who love him? But you have dishonored the poor man.

JAMES 1:26-2:6

The book of James puts our feet on the ground. His definition of religion is often quoted. It is what the logician calls a definition by illustration. Really, everything that he says may be regarded as illustrations of religion. One is *not* religious if he fails to control his tongue. That is, his religion is superficial and ineffective. The world needs religion that carries with it a deep concern for human suffering, poverty, inequality of opportunity, unjust social policies, and needless strife. This was perceived by John Oxenham:

> Blessed are the faithful strong,
>   They are the right hands of God.
> Blessed are they that dwell in peace,—
>   If they forget not God.
> Blessed are they that fight for the Right,
>   They shall save their souls,
>   For God is with them.

There is no virtue in being poor—nor in being rich. Virtue is the practice of justice and mercy, whatever the circumstances may be.

O GOD OUR FATHER, take from us all hypocrisy and incline our hearts toward kindness. Amen.

88 SHARING GOD

HINDUISM

> *He who dwells*
> *United with Brahman,*
> *Calm in mind,*
> *Not grieving, not craving,*
> *Regarding all men*
> *With equal acceptance:*
> *He loves me most dearly.*
>
> *To love is to know me,*
> *My innermost nature,*

The truth that I am:
Through this knowledge he enters
At once into my being.

BHAGAVAD-GITA 18.54-55

Union with God through an experience that is at once intellectual, emotional, and volitional is here set forth as an ideal. To be one with God is to be free from both grief and craving and to have no prejudices against any man. Through love one comes to know the innermost nature of God. The ideal of truth and goodness, embodied in the spirit of God, is without end. May we not truly be greater if we try to realize fully our relation to God as we come in contact with our fellows?

Separation from God, as here understood, is the essence of sin. Union with him is the bliss of salvation.

O GOD, save us from the sins of instability, craving, hatred, and ignorance, which separate us from thy being. Amen.

89   FOR THE MASTER'S SAKE

HINDUISM

Whatever man gives me
In true devotion:
Fruit or water,
A leaf, a flower:
I will accept it.
That gift is love,
His heart's dedication.

Whatever your action,
Food or worship:

101

> *Whatever the gift*
> *That you give to another:*
> *Whatever your vow*
> *To the work of the spirit:*
> *O son of Kunti,*
> *Lay these also*
> *As offerings before me.*

ьHAGAVAD-GITA 9.26-27

Another superb passage from the Gita, this one suggests the power of personalized religion. Krishna, a divine incarnation or avatar, is here speaking to his friend, the knight Arjuna. "For Lord Krishna's sake" is a phrase which would describe the motivation of many a devout Hindu who reads his "Song of God." It is hard to get away from personal religion, and why should we want to? Reality at times seems intensely personal, as motivation most often is.

Little acts of kindness, in all sincerity, would seem to qualify as a gift of love to God as he is known through his prophets or servants. Do we ever think about meeting God in such simple relationships of life? Is he not there?

O PERFECT LOVE, accept our love through human service. Make clear thine image in our lives together. Amen.

90 RESPONSE TO GOD'S GOODNESS

ISLAM

In the Name of God, the Compassionate, the Merciful.
By the noon-day BRIGHTNESS,
And by the night when it darkeneth!
Thy Lord hath not forsaken thee, neither hath he hated thee.
And surely the Future shall be better for thee than the Present,

And thy Lord shall assuredly be bounteous to thee and thou be
  satisfied.
Did he not find thee an orphan and provide thee a home?
And he found thee erring and guided thee,
And found thee needy and enriched thee.
As to the orphan therefore wrong him not;
And as to him that asketh of thee, chide him not away;
And as for the favors of thy Lord, tell them then abroad.

KORAN 93

Muhammad had been left an orphan and through God's grace had found a home with kindly relatives. His uncle, no doubt, had taught him the simple rules of faith and conduct, so that the boy came to feel that he had found happiness under the bounty and direction of Allah. Then it occurred to him most naturally: Since God had been good to him in his need, why should he not be kind to others in their need? Since God had enriched him, why should he not strive to enrich others? Especially should he help the orphans. Moreover, he should tell everyone of God's goodness to him. It is possible to do this inoffensively, modestly, and sincerely. In these ways we respond to God's goodness to us.

Not all fare so well as Muhammad. But even in catastrophe we must not think that God is expressing personal displeasure, for God is all goodness.

GIVER OF LIFE, may we reveal thy loving-kindness through our benevolence to others. May our own misfortunes teach us to understand and be helpful to others in their need. Amen.

Never in this world can hatred be stilled by hatred; it will be stilled only by non-hatred—this is the Law Eternal.

DHAMMAPADA 5

Although it is doubtful if the Buddha was the actual author of all the words of the Dhammapada, yet they are so regarded by the faithful. They have the same influence in the lives of Buddhists as if they were Buddha's own authoritative words. They govern their lives by such precepts as these. God's witness is present in other cultures than our own, urging people to overcome hatred by love and amity. The difficulty lies in observing the precept.

It takes some insight to perceive that hatred yields little personal satisfaction and much strife, while love and reconciliation bring peace and happiness to all.

AUTHOR OF PEACE, may we try sincerely and earnestly to win all people, even our enemies, to love and friendship through the manifestation of our own good will. Amen.

Let a man overcome anger by non-anger (gentleness), let him overcome evil by good, let him overcome the miser by liberality, let him overcome the liar by truth. DHAMMAPADA 223

The idea of overcoming evil by good is expressed in many religions but is practiced by few. No doctrine is more practical in human experience than this one. Anger is a sign of frustration. If the reaction to anger is anger, that just leads to more frustration. Gentleness points the way to compromise and friendship. Similarly liberality becomes catching and is likely to create altruistic sentiment in the miser. A liar may become ashamed of himself when others, clearly recognizing his lies, nevertheless speak to him truthfully.

Returning good for evil is an experiment that seems worth trying more often.

GOD HELP US to increase the good in the world by responding to anger by gentleness, to deceit by truthfulness, to selfishness by generosity. Amen.

93 TECHNIQUE OF GOOD WILL

"He abused me, he struck me, he overcame me, he robbed me"
—in those who harbor such thoughts hatred will never cease.
"He abused me, he struck me, he overcame me, he robbed me"
—in those who do not harbor such thoughts hatred will cease.

DHAMMAPADA 3-4

Let us live happily then, hating none in the midst of men who
hate. Let us dwell free from hate among men who hate.

DHAMMAPADA 197

Such passages help us to understand why Buddhism is sometimes referred to as a religion of ethical culture. It provides techniques for the realization of good will. One of the commonest of human experiences is the fact that good friends, brothers and sisters, even parents and children—people of truly noble character—nevertheless become estranged from one another through a chain of events for which neither is wholly responsible. Each remembers how the other behaved or spoke and will not forgive. Meanwhile the sands of time run out, and the sweetness of human kindness remains untasted. Against this sort of behavior the Buddha said, "Let us live happily . . . hating none."

It is strange how innocent and blameless each seems in his own eyes. Reconciliation will never be gained by maintaining one's own innocence as against another's guilt.

GOD OF PEACE, may we so learn the techniques of good will that we shall form cheerful habits and dispositions toward all. Amen.

106

To set up love, it is for you to love your relations; to set up respect, it is for you to respect your elders. The commencement is in the family and the State; the consummation is in all within the four seas.   SHU CHING 4.4.2

Francis H. Bradley goes so far as to say, "The heart is an idle abstraction; we are not to think of it, nor must we look at our insides, but at our work and our life, and say to ourselves, Am I fulfilling my appointed function or not? Fulfill it we can, if we will." Certainly there is a universal tendency to put much emotion and abstraction into our ideals. It is all well and good to love the Malaysians of Borneo and to feel sorry for the low castes of India. But there is little that we can do for them. The ones whom we can help most are near at hand. Closest are the members of our family. Then come those of the community and beyond. If we have no compassion for those closest to us, little good will come of our emotions for those far away. In today's world we must realize our duties to those half way round the globe. But we must begin with our own families and close neighbors.

There may be some who seem not to merit our love. Perhaps they are the very ones who need it most.

O GOD, may we be humble enough to begin building the kingdom of love in our own homes and communities. Amen.

If you love those who love you, what credit is that to you? For even sinners love those who love them. And if you do good to those who do good to you, what credit is that to you? For even sinners do the same. And if you lend to those from whom you hope to receive, what credit is that to you? Even sinners lend to sinners, to receive as much again. But love your enemies, and do good, and lend, expecting nothing in return; and your reward will be great, and you will be sons of the Most High; for he is kind to the ungrateful and the selfish. Be merciful, even as your Father is merciful. LUKE 6:32-36

It is amazing how much reciprocity there is in the world. We love those who love us and hate those who hate us. We "polish the apple" for those from whom we hope to receive something and snub those who snub us. Such behavior is most natural. It deserves no praise. There is nothing especially wrong with the kind of reciprocity that consists in the exchange of favors. Socrates noted the error of the other kind of reciprocity when in conversation with Polymarchus he asked, "Can the good harm anyone?" "Impossible." "And the just is the good?" "Certainly." "Then to injure a friend or anyone else is not the act of a just man, but of the opposite . . . the unjust?" Truly good people will not return evil for evil. Nor are they satisfied merely to exchange favors. Those who want to realize the divine image in their hearts will, like their heavenly Father, be kind even to the ungrateful and the selfish. They will be merciful, for God is merciful.

Perhaps we cannot suppress a feeling of resentment toward those who mistreat us. We can, however, transform that feeling into the fellowship of love.

HEAVENLY FATHER, grant that the thought of thy divine perfection may abide in our hearts as a constant inspiration to be like thee. Amen.

96 THE STRUCTURE OF GOODNESS

MOISM

(A disciple) said to Mo-ti: "Though you love universally the world cannot be said to be benefited; though I do not love (universally) the world cannot be said to be injured. Since neither of us has accomplished anything, what makes you then praise yourself and blame me?" Mo-ti answered: "Suppose a conflagration is on. One person is fetching water to extinguish it, and another is holding some fuel to reinforce it. Neither of them has yet accomplished anything, but which one do you value?" The disciple answered that he approved of the intention of the person who fetches water and disapproved of the intention of the person who holds fuel.

MO-TZŬ

Everything must have a proper structure if it is to accomplish its purpose: buildings, cities, governments, human bodies, philosophy. Goodness needs a suitable structure also, and it seems that love should be the motivating foundation of that structure. So thought Mo-Tzŭ (Mo Ti), an opponent of Confucianism. He insisted that universal love was not a bit impractical. Said he, "When feudal lords love one another there will be no more war; when heads of houses love one another there will be no more mutual usurpation; when individuals love one another there will be no more mutual injury. When ruler and ruled love each other they will be gracious and loyal; when father and son love each other they will be affectionate and filial; when elder and younger brothers love each other they will be harmonious. When all the people in the world love one another, then the strong will not overpower the weak, the many will not oppress the few, the wealthy will not mock the poor, the honored will not disdain the humble, and the cunning will not deceive the simple."

Mo-Tzŭ never dreamed of nuclear war. Should such arise, love could accomplish little. Love must prevent it from arising.

GOD GIVE US more faith in the power of love. May our love be without limit, reflecting the love of God. Amen.

97 BEING GENEROUS

> *Requite anger with virtue.*   TAO TÊ CHING 63
>
> *Return love for great hatred.*
> *Otherwise, when a great hatred is reconciled,*
>   *some of it will surely remain.*
> *How can this end in goodness?*   TAO TÊ CHING 79
>
> *Alike to good and bad*
> *I must be good,*
> *For Virtue is goodness.*
> *To honest folk*
> *And those dishonest ones*
> *Alike, I proffer faith.*
> *For Virtue is faithful.*   TAO TÊ CHING 49

One wonders what it was in the experience of the legendary founder of Taoism that led him to state the doctrine of generosity so forcefully. He seemed utterly convinced of the practicability of returning love for hatred, kindness for anger, and good faith for dishonesty. His logic was the logic of Socrates, namely, that unkindness is vicious, whether directed toward a good or a bad man. Good people do not want to increase the amount of evil in the world, so they will not resort to hatred under any circumstances.

The so-called "visionaries" who believe in loving their enemies are, in simple truth, the ones whose vision is clear enough to perceive the realities of logic and experience.

O God, may our hearts be large enough to harbor generous thoughts and motives toward our enemies as toward our friends. May we be zealous for the increase of total good. Amen.

98 THE COURAGE OF SELFLESS CHOICE

OLD TESTAMENT

And Lot, who went with Abram, also had flocks and herds and tents, so that the land could not support both of them dwelling together; for their possessions were so great that they could not dwell together, and there was strife between the herdsmen of Abram's cattle and the herdsmen of Lot's cattle. . . .
Then Abram said to Lot, "Let there be no strife between you and me, and between your herdsmen and my herdsmen; for we are kinsmen. Is not the whole land before you? Separate yourself from me. If you take the left hand, then I will go to the right; or if you take the right hand, then I will go to the left." And Lot lifted up his eyes, and saw that the Jordan valley was well watered everywhere like the garden of the Lord, like the land of Egypt in the direction of Zoar. . . . So Lot chose for himself all the Jordan valley. GENESIS 13:5-12

111

Universal love does not stand alone. It requires the support of unselfish choice and great courage. If a simple emotion were all that is necessary, then the world could be saved without sacrifice. But this is not the case, for life cannot be lived without conflict of interests, and in those conflicts great character is made—or lost. Children who grow up knowing only to choose for their own selfish interests are poorly nurtured. Men and women whose main concern is to see to it that no one gets the better of them turn out to be poor indeed. Generous motives need cultivating; they do not come easily. But either our prophets were all wrong, or we owe it to ourselves to be generous to others— and this is just one of the many paradoxes of life. Abram chose to be the least, but in that choice became the greatest, blest by God eternally.

Is there any real conflict between our resolution to prefer others above ourselves and our determination to excel in character? When we cultivate personal excellence, is it in the spirit of competitive rivalry with others? Or do we wish others to be as great, spiritually, as we strive to be?

ETERNAL JUDGE, may courage never fail us in our times of great decision. May we sincerely love our fellow man in the concrete situations of life. Amen.

99 THE GOOD NEIGHBOR

NEW TESTAMENT

But he, desiring to justify himself, said to Jesus, "And who is my neighbor?" Jesus replied, "A man was going down from Jerusalem to Jericho, and he fell among robbers, who stripped him and beat him, and departed, leaving him half-dead. Now by chance a priest was going down that road; and when he saw him he passed by on the other side. So likewise a Levite, when he came to the place and saw him, passed by on the other side. But a Samaritan, as he journeyed, came to where he was; and when he saw him, he had compassion, and went to him and bound up his wounds, pouring on oil and wine; then he set him on his own beast and brought him to an inn, and took care of him. And the next day he took out two denarii and gave them to the innkeeper, saying, 'Take care of him; and whatever more you spend, I will repay you when I come back.' Which of these three, do you think, proved neighbor to the man who fell among the robbers?" He said, "The one who showed mercy on him." And Jesus said to him, "Go and do likewise." LUKE 10:29-37

This is undoubtedly one of the greatest passages in all scriptures. It is great because in it universal love is applied to a universal situation. Not a word was said about loving those who hate you, and it may be that the man whom the Samaritan befriended was not his enemy. But that is irrelevant. It was the man's desperate need that beckoned the Samaritan to be a good neighbor. Sometimes our enemies need us more than our friends do; sometimes our friends need us most. But whoever needs us, to him it is our privilege to become a good neighbor. Neighborliness is realized only in life situations where we can be of service to others. In such situations we are prone to pass by on the other side.

It may seem that we can do very little when millions of the people of the world are desperately poor, sick, and discouraged. But what we can do, we ought to do.

O GOD, open our eyes to see the needs that are awaiting neighborly attention throughout the world. Create in us the spirit of compassion. Amen.

If I speak in the tongues of men and of angels, but have not love, I am a noisy gong or a clanging cymbal. And if I have prophetic powers, and understand all mysteries and all knowledge, and if I have all faith, so as to remove mountains, but have not love, I am nothing. If I give away all I have, and if I deliver my body to be burned, but have not love, I gain nothing.

Love is patient and kind; love is not jealous or boastful; it is not arrogant or rude. Love does not insist on its own way; it is not irritable or resentful; it does not rejoice at wrong, but rejoices in the right. Love bears all things, believes all things, hopes all things, endures all things.

Love never ends; as for prophecy, it will pass away; as for tongues, they will cease; as for knowledge, it will pass away. For our knowledge is imperfect and our prophecy is imperfect; but when the perfect comes, the imperfect will pass away. When I was a child, I spoke like a child, I thought like a child, I reasoned like a child; when I became a man, I gave up childish ways. For now we see in a mirror dimly, but then face to face. Now I know in part; then I shall understand fully, even as I have been fully understood. So faith, hope, love abide, these three; but the greatest of these is love.   1 CORINTHIANS 13:1-13

Wisdom is limited by experience and natural endowment. A loving disposition may shine brightly from even a child. Any teacher knows that students differ in their capacity to learn. But the poorest students are sometimes the ones best equipped with good will and the desire to serve. The Stoics regarded all men as God's children because all shared in universal reason. St. Paul found love to be the bond that united the family of God. No passage in world literature describes love with such insight as St. Paul's second paragraph above, yet no passage is so neglected in practice.

We need all the wisdom we can get. We need faith, and we cannot live without hope. But it is still true that the greatest virtue is love.

O PERFECT LOVE, may we make thee our master by dedicating ourselves to the spirit of love in all that we do. Amen.

101 THE SUPERIOR MAN

MOISM

To be a superior man one should take care of his friend as he does of himself, and take care of his friend's parents as his own. Therefore when he finds his friend hungry he would feed him, and when he finds him cold he would clothe him. In his sickness he would serve him, and when he is dead he would bury him.

MO-TZŬ

In this passage a great Chinese prophet condemned selfishness in friendship. We may as well admit that many of our acts of friendship are basically selfish. A friend does something for us; we do something equal for him. If he does not respond, we cease to be active friends. Mo-Tzŭ placed friendship on a higher plane. He expanded the concept of the family beyond the biological frame. Whatever we feel that we ought to do for members of our own family, that we should be willing to do for friends when they need us. Most acts of friendship are rewarding in some sense. It takes a superior man to perform acts for friends without any thought of rewards of any kind.

To treat others as they treat us is a rule as old as Moses. To treat them as we would like to be treated is the rule of love.

O God, may our benevolence transcend our selfishness and our hope of reward. May we regard service as a privilege of friendship, not merely an obligation. God make us truly superior. Amen.

102 THE SENSE OF VALUES

TAOISM

> *Hard-pressed, from serving other men,*
> *He has enough and some to spare;*
> *But having given all he had,*
> *He then is very rich indeed.*
>
> TAO TÊ CHING 81
>
> *Given compassion, I can take courage;*
> *Given frugality, I can abound;*
> *If I can be the world's most humble man,*
> *Then I can be its highest instrument.*
>
> TAO TÊ CHING 67

The truest insights in the world are paradoxes. Here are some of them from the Tao Tê Ching. We need a keen sense of values in order to appreciate them. The first quotation means that the most contented people are those who serve gladly and give generously, rather than those who by nature demand service of others and cling to all their possessions as if they were their souls. In the second quotation we read first that true courage lies not in boldly fighting others, but in daring to believe in them, to understand them, and to help them. Then we read that abundance consists in having few wants. Since real happiness comes from an inner principle, we can free ourselves from dependence on wealth, which alone has never made anyone happy. Finally, the humblest man can do the most good in the world—which should give courage to all good people.

Sincerity is the first prerequisite of a sound sense of values.

God, give us the wealth of benevolence and the strength of humility. Help us to cultivate the insights of paradox, that we may experience a true sense of values. Amen.

103 HOW TO BE EXALTED

JUDAISM

(Rabbi Nechumah) had never striven to exalt his own standing by lowering that of his neighbor. This was agreeable to the example set by Rabbi Hunna, for the latter, while bearing on his shoulders a heavy spade, was met by Rabbi Choana Ben Chanilai, who, considering the burden derogatory to the dignity of so great a man, insisted upon relieving him of the implement and carrying it himself. But Rabbi Hunna refused, saying, "Were this your habitual calling I might permit it, but I certainly shall not permit another to perform an office which, if done by myself, may be looked upon by some as menial."

Secondly, he had never gone to his night's rest with a heart harboring ill will against his fellow man, conformably with the practice of Mar Zutra, who, before sleeping, offered this prayer: "O Lord! forgive all those who have done me injury."   TALMUD

The most common motive for unkind criticism is in order to show the relative superiority of the critic. To say, "That fellow is stupid," is to imply that the speaker is smart.

Rabbi Hunna would not accept this kind of self-exaltation. Rabbi Hunna was a great man, but he considered it no indignity to carry a heavy spade. To allow his fellow rabbi to relieve him of the burden would be to imply both that the carrying of the burden was intrinsically undignified and that his fellow rabbi was less worthy of dignity than himself. Rabbi Hunna also practiced that excellent habit of clearing the slate of any ill will before going to sleep at night. Others might bear him ill will, but that was their responsibility; his was to make his own heart pure.

We must wonder what it is in human nature that makes people take pleasure in exalting themselves by lowering the standing of their neighbors. Our own society leaped forward when we realized that the prosperity of the many would not militate against the wealth of the few. Dignity, like prosperity, should not depend on denying the same to others.

O GOD, help us to harbor only good will toward our neighbors, not insisting that we be more highly esteemed than they. May we possess the forgiving spirit. Amen.

104 HOW TO SERVE GOD

NEW TESTAMENT

Then the King will say to those at his right hand, "Come, O blessed of my Father, inherit the kingdom prepared for you from the foundation of the world; for I was hungry and you gave me food, I was thirsty and you gave me drink, I was a stranger and you welcomed me, I was naked and you clothed me, I was sick and you visited me, I was in prison and you came to me." Then the righteous will answer him, "Lord, when did we see thee hun-

*gry and feed thee, or thirsty and give thee drink? And when did
we see thee a stranger and welcome thee, or naked and clothe
thee? And when did we see thee sick or in prison and visit thee?"
And the King will answer them, "Truly, I say to you, as you
did it to one of the least of these my brethren, you did it to me."*
                                          MATTHEW 25:34-40

The deepest religious insights are those which stress plain
human kindness. So unaffected was the compassion of the
heirs of the kingdom that they were unaware of it. All that
they had done was, out of pity, to help the poor, the sick,
and the imprisoned. We may feel that it is religiously unimportant to be kind to strangers or help those in need.
Such was not Jesus' judgment. Christian missions came to
mean more to those of other lands when we introduced hos-
pitals, schools, and scientific agriculture. No wonder, for
the people then realized that we were interested in their
troubles, not merely in some abstract theory of salvation.

The solution of people's problems is an integral part of
their salvation. We need to realize the eternal importance
of the everyday needs of everyday people.

GOD OF OUR SALVATION, may we have eyes to see thee suffering in the streets and hidden places of our communities
for the want of our human compassion. Amen.

105 FILIAL DUTY

CONFUCIANISM

*The duties of universal obligation are five . . . those between
sovereign and minister, between father and son, between husband
and wife, between elder brother and younger, and those belonging
to the intercourse of friends.*   DOCTRINE OF THE MEAN
What are "the things which men consider right"? Kindness on

119

the part of the father, and filial duty on that of the son; gentle-
ness on the part of the elder brother, and obedience on that of
the younger; righteousness on the part of the husband, and sub-
mission on that of the wife; kindness on the part of the elders,
and deference on that of juniors; with benevolence on the part
of the ruler, and loyalty on that of the minister;—these ten are
the things which men consider to be right.   LI CHI

The Chinese tried to organize their thinking about morality and came up with the doctrine of the fivefold relationship of life. There is some variation in the telling of those
relationships, but the essence is the Confucian doctrine of
filial piety. There can be no harmony in the home or community unless the principle of responsibility is recognized.
Not that the father's power should be arbitrary, for even
age makes mistakes. Yet there is a certain wisdom in the
experience of age, and sons would do well to seek the
guidance of loving parents—and let us include the feminine
side of this picture. In our democratic framework, maybe
the father, husband, and elder brother should not always
make the final decisions. In all relationships, however, reli-
ance is on the wisdom of experience, tempered by kindness,
gentleness, righteousness, and benevolence. Filial loyalty is
still a needed virtue—east and west.

In view of the grave dangers facing us today, democracy
must find ways to cultivate a proper regard for the authority of wisdom and experience.

GOD MAKE US more faithful to the real values of family
discipline, with due regard for democratic values. May we
seek benevolent guidance from the wisdom of experience
and exercise the power of wisdom when it becomes our responsibility. Amen.

If a man has a good friend to resist him in doing bad actions, he will have his reputation preserved; so if a father has a son to resist his wrong commands, he will be saved from committing serious faults.

When the command is wrong, a son should resist his father, and a minister should resist his august master.

The maxim is, "Resist when wrongly commanded." Hence how can he be called filial who obeys his father when he is commanded to do wrong?   THE BOOK OF FILIAL DUTY, 15

It is not always right for children to obey their parents, nor for wives to submit to their husbands, nor subjects to rulers (Colossians 3:18-25). As human life is complex, so rules must be complex. Exceptions to the general rule should be in accordance with the purpose of the rule, namely, to bring all acts into harmony with the wisdom of experience. Unfortunately, people who have authority are likely to exercise it even when their wisdom does not justify it. In such cases we are morally obligated to resist—whether the authority be a husband, a father, a priest, or a ruler. When disobedience is a moral obligation, it ceases to be a vice.

All the great religions support St. Peter's declaration that "We must obey God rather than men."

O GOD, give us courage to resist our friends and those in positions of authority when we know that they are seriously in the wrong. At all other times, keep us humbly obedient to the counsels of wisdom in those whose part it is to lead. Amen.

OLD TESTAMENT

Then the Lord God said, "It is not good that the man should be alone; I will make him a helper fit for him." . . . *So the Lord God caused a deep sleep to fall upon the man, and while he slept took one of his ribs and closed up its place with flesh; and the rib which the Lord God had taken from the man he made into a woman and brought her to the man. Then the man said,*
"This at last is bone of my bones and flesh of my flesh;
she shall be called Woman, because she was taken out of Man."
Therefore a man leaves his father and his mother and cleaves to his wife, and they become one flesh. GENESIS 2:18, 21-24

Primitive man was trying to understand why the husband and wife relationship was so definitive and complete. He used this story to express his intuition. It became a symbol of his conviction that the marriage relationship was sacred, divinely ordained. And so it is. But man is both organismic and spiritual, and the union of man and wife must be both physical and spiritual if it is to realize the divine purpose. Unhappy is he whose total personality was not involved in his marriage choice. Many of the ills of society are due to immaturity of romantic reflection. What is the cure? Recognition of the necessity of spiritual adjustment. No spiritual progress can be made by either party without frankly recognizing the sacredness of the marriage relationship and its requirement of spiritual as well as organic union.

God and nature cannot be at odds. Blessed are they in whom spirit is the principle of unity.

LOVER OF ALL MANKIND, may we perceive thy presence in the complete mingling of two spirits whose supreme aim is righteousness and compassion. May the lonely find God in a life that is wholly given to the beauty of kindly service. Amen.

108   THE GOOD WIFE

OLD TESTAMENT

A good wife who can find?
   She is far more precious than jewels.
The heart of her husband trusts in her,
   and he will have no lack of gain.
She does him good, and not harm,
   all the days of her life.
She seeks wool and flax
   and works with willing hands.

.   .   .   .

She opens her hand to the poor,
   and reaches out her hands to the needy.

.   .   .   .

She looks well to the ways of her household,
   and does not eat the bread of idleness.
Her children rise up and call her blessed;
   her husband also, and he praises her:
"Many women have done excellently,
   but you surpass them all."

PROVERBS 31:10-13, 20, 27-29

Why does the Bible not contain a panegyric to the good husband? Probably because it was written by men instead of women. If there were such a poem to the good husband, it might start out in the same way, substituting husband for wife. In any case, it is well for the husband or wife to contemplate the excellent qualities of the other and to give

123

expression to any positive conclusions. The tendency too often is to see the other's imperfections as each seeks his own separate goals. Life can be beautiful if we practice appreciation of our companions in life—whether in marriage or in friendship—and everyone must have friends.

Some of the qualities for which the good wife is praised in this passage are thrift, efficiency, initiative, charity, providence, faithfulness, and dignity. Charm and beauty are said to be relatively unimportant.

O GOD, help us to appreciate those who are nearest and dearest to us and to strive for perfection in our familial relationship. Amen.

109 VALUES OF FRIENDSHIP

OLD TESTAMENT

And she said, "See, your sister-in-law has gone back to her people and to her gods; return after your sister-in-law." But Ruth said, "Entreat me not to leave you or to return from following you; for where you go I will go, and where you lodge I will lodge; your people shall be my people, and your God my God; where you die I will die, and there will I be buried. May the Lord do so to me and more also if even death parts me from you." RUTH 1:15-17

Here is a case of strong friendship between a young woman and her mother-in-law. The experience of friendship contains a strong element of emotional dependence, as Ruth depended on Naomi. She might have declared her independence and chosen to live with the Moabites. But something about Naomi had impressed Ruth with the fact that here was a woman of strength and courage, a woman whose love for her husband and her sons was benevolent and outgoing and whose grief was sincere but sane. She knew by instinct that her friendship offered consolation and encouragement. She must go with her to the land of Joseph. On the other side, Naomi needed friendship too. Ruth filled her exact need by affording her an opportunity to employ her special fitness to console and encourage the younger woman. Friendships depend not upon equivalent age or common circumstance, but on complementary needs and opportunities.

There can be no true friendship between self-centered people, though there is always mutual profit in true friendship.

O GOD, may we realize more fully the spiritual potentialities of friendship with our associates. As we need friends, so we would be friends. Amen.

110 CHOOSING FRIENDS

NEW TESTAMENT

And as he sat at table in his house, many tax collectors and sinners were sitting with Jesus and his disciples; for there were many who followed him. And the scribes of the Pharisees, when they saw that he was eating with sinners and tax collectors, said to his disciples, "Why does he eat with tax collectors and sinners?" And when Jesus heard it, he said to them, "Those who are well have no need of a physician, but those who are sick; I came not to call the righteous, but sinners." MARK 2:15-17

Jesus did not justify his friendship with sinners by saying that they were as good as anyone else, but by pointing out that they needed salvation. Blessed are those whose charac-

ters are such that they can associate with sinners blame-
lessly. The world needs more of them. Not all should choose
their friends for the sake of lifting them to a higher level.
Many people ought frankly to seek friends who can
strengthen and encourage them in the good life. Such a motive is worthy for most of us. Only he who has a great
vision, whose strong springs of action come from within,
can afford to have friends who are sinners.

Intergroup friendships, as between people of different
nationalities, are often a challenge to spiritual growth.

O God, take away our vanity but give us firm possession
of the inner principle, that we may make friends blame-
lessly with all, humbly seeking not so much our own good
as theirs. Amen.

111 THE DUTY OF MAN

JUDAISM

*Upon one occasion an unbeliever approached Shammai and
mockingly requested the Rabbi to teach to him the tenets and
principles of Judaism in the space of time he could stand on one
foot. Shammai, in great wrath, bade him begone, and the man
then applied to Hillel, who said,*

*"Do not unto others what you would not have others do to
you. This is the whole law; the rest, merely commentaries upon
it."* TALMUD

It is good to know that all the major religions of mankind
share the insight of the golden rule. It was stated by Hillel,
a pre-Christian rabbi, as by Jesus soon afterward. The
ancient Mahabharata of Hinduism stated, "This is the sum
of duty: Do naught unto others which would cause you

pain if done to you." Confucius said that there is one maxim that may always be applied: "What you do not want done to yourself, do not do to others." He also said, "Now the man of perfect virtue, wishing to be established himself, seeks also to establish others; wishing to be enlarged himself, he seeks also to enlarge others." According to the Traditions, Muhammad said, "No one of you is a believer until he loves for his brother what he loves for himself." The Buddhist version: "Hurt not others in ways that you yourself would find hurtful." And so it seems that good men everywhere have discovered this rule of the association between people, as also the rules of addition and subtraction.

If all men everywhere admit the golden rule, it is all the more strange that everywhere they break it. The ideal remains like a guiding star.

O GOD, may we have pure hearts and kind thoughts at all times, lest we too fail to follow the golden rule. May we be as concerned for our own spiritual perfection as we think others should be for theirs. Amen.

112   WHENCE COMES CONTENTMENT?

CONFUCIANISM

In the morning, hear the Way; in the evening, die content.
ANALECTS 4.8

These words seem like sweet singing under a cloudy sky. So many people today live in fear and want while others become cynical and disgusted with life, that words like these are greatly needed. They suggest that life could be a paradise if everyone were to learn the Way as he grows into adulthood. Then after a good, peaceful life, without fear or hate, with an understanding family and helpful friends, he would find death to be the concluding note of a symphony— which needs to be finished. Confucius actually had about as many disappointments in life as any of us. Yet he was able to find contentment in his knowledge of the way of truth and goodness. Many more like him have been able to achieve contentment, despite all odds.

The challenging thought is that all human beings could live such lives, if they but understood.

O God, help us to realize that the good life is the most desirable life. Give us the spirit of contentment in the knowledge of the way everlasting. Amen.

113 FORTHRIGHT LIVING

CONFUCIANISM

The great man does not think before hand of his words that they may be sincere, nor of his actions that they may be resolute; he simply speaks and does what is right.   MENCIUS 4

There has been some controversy about the value of consistency. Said William Allen White, "Consistency is a paste jewel that only cheap men cherish." Emerson said, "A foolish consistency is the hobgoblin of little minds, adored by little statesmen and philosophers and divines." Neither writer meant to make a virtue of inconsistency. The trouble is that our vision is so limited that what is consistent within its limits may need correction in the larger view. Consistency must be regarded as a virtue. But the final test of consistency must be the realities of experience. We must always be willing to face new facts, even if doing so makes us change our point of view so that we seem to be inconsistent with our former selves. The "great man" who does not plan his words and actions ahead of time, with a view to consistency, must surely live according to a fundamental philosophy which makes all his actions right, and therefore consistent.

There are times when the most earnest people despair of knowing what is the right course to follow. This is no simple problem.

GOD OF WISDOM, make us forthright in our way of living. But give us first the patience to form a sound philosophy of life. Amen.

114 THE HUMILITY OF WISDOM

ANCIENT EGYPT

Be not arrogant because of thy knowledge, and be not puffed up for that thou art a learned man. Take counsel with the ignorant as with the learned. . . . Goodly discourse is more hidden than the precious greenstone, and yet it is found with slave-girls over the millstones. PROVERBS OF PTAHHOTEP

Ptahhotep, a grand vizier of the Egyptian Fifth Dynasty, is supposed to have spoken these words to his son about forty-five hundred years ago. Ptahhotep realized that an education does not always educate and that the uneducated are often quite perceptive of human values. He understood that the truly wise are neither arrogant nor snobbish. Distinctions of education and class sometimes bring us in contact with educated bores while denying us contact with common people of genuine insight. Learning is a gateway to wisdom, and the truly wise are humble. Socrates, acclaimed as a wise man, knew how little he really knew. One cannot really learn much without first becoming humble.

Knowledge is always better than ignorance, but intellectual snobbery ignores the responsible role of wisdom.

GOD FREE US from arrogance and pride and give us perceptive hearts, that we may recognize greatness in unexpected places. May we seek wisdom not for snobbish reasons, but for its intrinsic human value. Amen.

115 FINDING TEACHERS

He who finds instructors for himself comes to the supreme dominion; he who says that others are not equal to himself comes to ruin.   SHU CHING 4.2.4

It is remarkable how many of the great religions have been founded by teachers or have had their traditions carried on by teachers. Jesus was the great "teacher of Galilee." The Buddha spent the last half of his life teaching his disciples. Judaism has been kept vital by a long tradition of rabbis. Confucius was pre-eminently a teacher, as was his later apostle Mencius. Confucianism caused the function of the teacher to be recognized by the emperors and the people of China. The simple inscription on Confucius' grave is ANCIENT, MOST HOLY TEACHER. Socrates consecrated and Plato exalted the role of the teacher. In modern times free public education is a tribute to the beneficence and power of teaching. It is impossible to estimate what great good has been done in the world by teaching. We need more and better teaching, especially in religion and the humanities. It might even be possible, by the right approach, to teach wisdom to those who say, like the Psalmist,

> I have more understanding than all my teachers.
>
> 119.99

We must never give up the hope that all can be taught how to live effectively.

One who cannot find or does not feel the need of teachers is really to be pitied.

GOD GIVE US due reverence for the great teachers of mankind. May we keep our minds and hearts open to new truth and new insights. When we teach, may we do so with preparation and power. Amen.

116 SPIRITUAL ENTERPRISE

CONFUCIANISM

The good in you I will not dare to keep concealed; and for the evil in me I will not dare to forgive myself. I will examine these things in harmony with the mind of God. SHU CHING 4.3.3
The great man is he who does not lose his child's-heart.

MENCIUS 4

One of the commonest human faults is to magnify one's own virtues and another's vice, or—which is the same thing —to conceal or minimize another's virtues and one's own vices. The theoretical basis of such behavior must be that we regard one another as rivals in virtue. But if that is the case, then certainly we do not promote our own goodness by falsely magnifying it while we minimize another's. Nor do we gain virtue by minimizing our vices while magnifying those of others. Of course, if what we are after is merely a good reputation, however unjustly gained, such behavior might be regarded as successful. Suffice it to say that this is not the virtuous course.

As Mencius said, the truly good man is one who throughout life maintains the simple straightforward manner of childhood.

GOD OF TRUTH, make us utterly realistic in viewing our own virtues and completely kind in viewing the faults of others. May we understand the greatness of humility. Amen.

117 THE BLESSED MEEK

TAOISM

The highest goodness is like water, for water is excellent in benefitting all things, and it does not strive. It occupies the lowest place, which men abhor. And therefore it is near akin to Tao.

TAO TÊ CHING 8

The Wise Man chooses to be last
And so becomes the first of all;
Denying self, he too is saved.

TAO TÊ CHING 7

The simile is excellent. Here is one principle by which we may live confidently: the principle of humility. The related principle is, Do not strive for the unnatural. Without striving, water seeks the lowest place and thereby benefits all.

It merely fulfills its own nature as a fluid obeying the law of gravity. So we, by humbly doing those things which we are fitted to do, will be fulfilling our God-given natures and thereby benefiting all people. This means that human nature is divinely ordained to live in a society with mutual helpfulness and understanding. If our natures are not that of the mere brute, but, as it were, of angels, it is yet God who has made us thus and not we ourselves, except to the extent that we will to will the good. Realizing this, we will not be vain.

Only the humble can learn; pride prevents us from realizing our need. Only those who realize their need can strive further for perfection. Pride offends those on whom we depend for human co-operation. It is the meek that shall inherit the earth.

GOD MAKE US HUMBLE, lest the offense of our pride bring misery. Make us humble, that we may serve and thereby live effectively. Amen.

118 QUIET STRENGTH

TAOISM

The softest of stuff in the world
Penetrates quickly the hardest;
Insubstantial, it enters
Where no room is.

TAO TÊ CHING 43

Nothing is weaker than water
But . . . nothing will alter its way.

TAO TÊ CHING 78

133

Humility is not weakness. The humble man possesses true strength, like water which penetrates the hardest substances. As said Isaiah,

> they who wait for the Lord shall renew their strength,
>   they shall mount up with wings like eagles,
> they shall run and not be weary,
>   they shall walk and not faint.

The strength which we seek is not the strength to lift a ton of marble; we seek the strength to overcome discouragement, to persist when the case seems hopeless, to differ when all others agree, to witness to unpopular truth. Only those who are truly humble have such strength.

> Teach us to care and not to care
> Teach us to sit still
> Even among these rocks,
> Our peace in His will.

"Humility is the most difficult of all virtues to achieve," wrote T. S. Eliot; "nothing dies harder than the desire to think well of oneself." Still, we need not think ill of ourselves in order to be humble. Self-respect is not the same as vanity.

GOD GIVE US the quiet strength that comes with inner consciousness of right, with motives pure, with dedication to what we believe with all our mind and heart. Amen.

When one by force subdues men, they do not submit to him in heart. They submit because their strength is not adequate to resist. When one subdues men by virtue, in their hearts' core they are pleased, and sincerely submit, as was the case with the seventy disciples in their submission to Confucius.   MENCIUS 2

Said Burke, "A nation is not governed, which is perpetually to be conquered." There can be no peace until men submit to governors willingly. The power of man over man is a necessary principle of social organization. The higher we climb the ladder of civilization, the more power our leaders have. George Washington's power was small compared with today's President. Such power should always be regarded as a sacred trust, entailing a heavy responsibility on the part of him who exercises the authority. Surely power does not justify pride or vain display. Lest it lead to vanity, let him who has power humbly seek the counsel of his enemies and all who will co-operate. Whatever the degree of our power, we must keep in mind the goal of the greatest justice and well-being of all.

The power of the teacher is ideal in that he uses only the virtue of truth as his means. Any great leader must adopt the way of a teacher.

O GOD, give us virtuous leaders, and may we give such leaders our fullest support. Whatever authority we may have, help us to exercise it with charity and every other virtue. Amen.

> *Wrong not, and ye shall not be wronged.*   KORAN 2:279
> *Let there be no injury in the world and no requital.* TRADITIONS
> *Turn away evil by what is better, and lo! he between whom and thyself was enmity, shall be as though he were a warm friend.*   KORAN 41:34
> *Whoso beareth wrongs with patience and forgiveth—this verily is a bounden duty.*   KORAN 42:41

Muslim tradition, no less than any other, requires that the believer shall be kind, sympathetic, generous, patient, and forgiving. Such insight is as universal as the golden rule. It may be said that when the believer of any tradition is unkind, it is not because his sacred scriptures teach him to be so. It is for the same reason that most of us are at times mean, unsympathetic, and retaliatory. When this is the case, we are simply being neglectful and unfaithful to our sacred commitments. The kind response is really the way of wisdom, for the unkind person only makes his enemies more bitter and alienates his friends. "What wisdom can you find that is greater than kindness?" demanded Rousseau.

The kind response in international and intergroupal relations is especially needed today.

GOD GIVE US INSIGHT into the hearts of our enemies, that we may perceive them as potential friends. May our enemies realize our fundamental good will. Amen.

Blessed is he whose transgression is forgiven,
   whose sin is covered.
Blessed is the man to whom the Lord imputes no iniquity,
   and in whose spirit there is no deceit.

When I declared not my sin, my body wasted away
   through my groaning all day long.
For day and night thy hand was heavy upon me;
   my strength was dried up as by the heat of summer.

I acknowledged my sin to thee,
   and I did not hide my iniquity;
I said, "I will confess my transgressions to the Lord":
   then thou didst forgive the guilt of my sin.

PSALM 32:1-5

Here is a word picture of a human soul that has caught a vision of its own imperfection against the background of the perfection that is God. It is a sign of spiritual progress when we become aware that our imperfections are really sins against God. Being created in the image of God, we ought to maintain the perfection of that image. When we fail, we really need divine forgiveness. If forgiveness is sought, divine grace is always ready. For God is merciful, desiring the reformation of the sinner rather than his condemnation. The realization of God's forgiving nature is one of the greatest inspirations of the Christian tradition, as it may be also of Judaism, Islam, Hinduism, Buddhism, and other traditions in which the concept of a holy and merciful God is cultivated.

137

Only the humble can pray for forgiveness. Only the humble can seek perfection.

GOD STRENGTHEN US in mind and heart as we engage in the quest for righteousness. When we sin, make us humble enough to confess our sins. May we harbor no secret faults through self-deceit. Amen.

122 THE INFLUENCE OF ONE

CONFUCIANISM

The decline and fall of a State may arise from one man. The glory and tranquility of a State may also arise from the goodness of one man.   SHU CHING 5.30

Edward Everett Hale summed up the importance of the individual when he wrote this poem for the Lend-a-Hand Society:

> I am only one,
> But still I am one.
> I cannot do everything,
> But still I can do something;
> And because I cannot do everything
> I will not refuse to do the something that I can do.

That "something" may prove to be most important. If it needs to be done, then all the world depends upon our doing it. Without that deed, the whole world would be different. It may be that the thing that needs most to be done is to say just the thing that we can say at the right time. As Thoreau put it: "Any man more right than his neighbor constitutes a majority of one."

Humility ceases to be a virtue when we belittle our own importance in carrying on the work of the world.

O GOD, give us self-confidence without vanity, that we may rightly evaluate the part that we can play in the building of thy kingdom on earth. Amen.

123 WHO IS PERFECT?

BUDDHISM

This is an old saying. . . . "They blame him who remains silent, they blame him who talks much, they blame also him who speaks in moderation." There is not anyone in the world who is not blamed.

There never was, nor will be, nor is there now to be found anyone who is (wholly) blamed, anyone who is (wholly) praised.

DHAMMAPADA 227-228

This tells us that people will criticize us regardless of what we do. Our task is to be restrained in the criticism of others, realizing that no one is perfect and also that no one is absolutely bad. There is some bad in the best of us and some good in the worst of us. We are prone to give universal condemnation to those people whom we find lacking in certain characteristics of virtue. If we knew them better, we should very likely find that those same people had more virtues than faults. The knowledge of our own faults should make us sympathetic with others who have faults along with their own virtues. If a perfect God loves both the (relatively) good and the (relatively) bad, then it would seem less than perfect for us to despise the bad.

There is no arrogance in goodness. The only way to grow better is by realizing our own imperfections.

FATHER OF US ALL, make us charitable toward others, while we rid ourselves of all self-righteousness. May we be patient when falsely accused. Amen.

124   THE FLAWS IN OURSELVES

BUDDHISM

Very easy is it to discover flaws in others, but very difficult to see one's own. One winnows the shortcomings of others like chaff, but one covers his own as a dishonest gambler covers a losing throw. .DHAMMAPADA 252

Here is an expression of a theme found in the Sermon on the Mount. The Dhammapada, from which the passage is taken, was probably written early in the third century B.C. The admonition to be charitable in one's judgment of others, considering one's own faults, is a pertinent piece of advice in all ages and places. By judging others harshly for their faults we implicitly assume that we do not have such faults ourselves. A more valid assumption is that none of us is perfect. The most critical people may be the very ones who try, perhaps unconsciously, to cover up their own faults by exposing the faults of others. There is a basic dishonesty about such behavior.

Faultfinding may not always be hypocritical; in some cases it may be a sort of mental illness which calls for kind and patient sympathy.

GOD GIVE US the grace to try to understand those people whom we are prone to criticize. May we judge ourselves by the same standards that we apply to our fellow men. Amen.

The Master said, In vain have I looked for a single man capable of seeing his own faults and bringing the charge home against himself. ANALECTS 5.26

The disease of men is this: that they neglect their own fields, and go to weed the fields of others, and that what they require from others is great, while what they lay upon themselves is light. MENCIUS VII

Tsu-kung was always criticising other people. The Master said, "It is fortunate for Tsu he is so perfect himself as to have time to spare for this. I myself have none." ANALECTS 14.31

One of the best answers to the charge of the corruption of any good thing by hypocrisy was given by La Rochefoucauld: "Hypocrisy is the homage that vice pays to virtue." Hypocrisy is a disease which affects us all to a greater or less degree, and in the interest of spiritual health we may as well face it. We can never overcome it unless we do. Everyone tends to behave as he is expected to do, whether he means it or not. In unimportant matters it may make little difference. But as a rule of life, it is important that we cultivate sincerity and that we pay more attention to the correction of our own faults than to the criticism of the faults of others.

One word of caution: It is not wrong to criticize others kindly and sympathetically. But this takes wisdom.

GOD GIVE US SYMPATHY for those who are morally sick. Help us to be the good physician. Amen.

You are the salt of the earth; but if salt has lost its taste, how shall its saltness be restored? It is no longer good for anything except to be thrown out and trodden under foot by men.

You are the light of the world. A city set on a hill cannot be hid. Nor do men light a lamp and put it under a bushel, but on a stand, and it gives light to all in the house. Let your light so shine before men, that they may see your good works and give glory to your Father who is in heaven.   MATTHEW 5:13-16

This passage should be read in the light of Jesus' teachings about hypocrisy. He told his disciples to practice their good deeds in private, not for the eyes of men but for the rewards of heaven. (Matthew 6:1-7.) There is really no contradiction between the two passages, for Jesus was concerned with motives. The hypocrites are insincere; they practice the forms of righteousness in order to gain the applause of men. On the other hand, those who are the salt of the earth and the light of the world behave as they do from a deep inner conviction. Their reward comes from within, from the sense of moral fitness, from the divine approval.

The insincerity of the hypocrites repels many from practices which may be perfectly good. The simple sincerity of the virtuous is to the good life like salt to the meal or light in the darkness.

GOD KEEP US SINCERE deep down in our hearts, but help us to check our conduct also by reference to social approval. In case of conflict, may we always prefer the divine witness. Amen.

Hail, thou whose strides are long, who comest forth from Heliopolis, I have not done iniquity. . . . I have not robbed with violence. . . . I have not committed theft. . . . I have not slain man or woman. . . . I have not made light the bushel. . . . I have not acted deceitfully. . . . I have not uttered falsehood. . . . I have not defiled the wife of a man. . . . I have not committed any sin against purity. . . . I have not struck fear into any man. . . . I have not been a man of anger. . . . I have not stirred up strife. . . . I have not judged hastily. . . . I have not multiplied my speech overmuch. . . . I have not sought for distinctions.

BOOK OF THE DEAD 125

These words represent the Egyptian conscience over thirty-five hundred years ago. And that conscience was keen. Here the departed soul stood in the presence of God and professed its innocence not only of the usual gross crimes, but also of unethical business relations (making light the bushel), deceitfulness, lying, impurity, unkindness (making people afraid), anger, troublemaking, immature judgment, garrulousness, and the desire for special consideration. In the setting of eternity, one's spiritual character may be seen in its true proportions.

Perhaps we have underestimated the moral capacity of ancient man and overestimated our own.

GOD HELP US to be completely honest, truthful, kind, and restrained in judgment and speech as we deal with our fellow men. May we strive for these qualities not through superstitious fear, but because of the simple attractiveness of such a life. Amen.

128 INDULGENCE AND DENIAL

BUDDHISM

*These two extremes, O monks, are not to be practised by one
who has gone forth from the world. What are the two? That
conjoined with the passions, low, vulgar, common, ignoble, and
useless, and that conjoined with self-torture, painful, ignoble, and
useless.*   SAMYUTTA-NIKAYA 5.420

These are the words of the Buddha in his First Sermon
at Benares. After a youth of pleasure, followed by six years
of self-torture in the wilderness, he had finally been enlightened. Two things he knew. One was that pleasure was
a superficial and unsatisfying kind of happiness. The other
was that peace of mind is no more to be achieved through
ascetic self-denial than through self-indulgence.

In principle Buddha did not mean to condemn the common pleasures of life enjoyed in moderation.

GOD HELP US truly to discriminate between the superficial
and the real in human satisfaction. Amen.

129 WORTHY SELF-DISCIPLINE

NEW TESTAMENT

*And he said to all, "If any man would come after me, let him
deny himself and take up his cross daily and follow me. For
whoever would save his life will lose it; and whoever loses his
life for my sake, he will save it. For what does it profit a man if
he gains the whole world and loses or forfeits himself?"*
                                                    LUKE 9:23-25

The self-centered life is really self-defeating. Only the life of kindly service satisfies. Taking up the cross means dedicating one's whole energies to worthiest goals. As even the Buddha said, self-denial simply for the sake of self-denial is profitless and foolish. But it is wisdom to deny ourselves of things which stand in the way of greater goals. This calls for intelligent self-discipline—a mode of behavior consistent with the principles of both Buddhism and Christianity, as well as most other religions.

There is no one—no one at all—who does not need to cultivate self-discipline as a means to self-realization.

GOD GRANT that we may not shun that self-discipline which is necessary to great accomplishment. May we not fear to lose ourselves in human service. Amen.

130 THE MIDDLE PATH

BUDDHISM

Avoiding these two extremes the Tathagata has gained the knowledge of the Middle Way, which gives sight and knowledge, and tends to calm, to insight, enlightenment, nirvana.

What, O monks, is the Middle Way, which gives sight . . . ? It is the Eightfold Path, namely, right views, right intention, right speech, right action, right livelihood, right effort, right mindfulness, right concentration. SAMYUTTA-NIKAYA 5.420

Oddly enough, the West remembers Buddha (the Tathagata: one who has "thus come") primarily for his doctrine of the painfulness of life and the need for renouncing our desires. But the Buddha's stress was upon moderation as

145

the way to wisdom and contentment. Such a life should be universally desired.

The Buddha's insight into the virtue of moderation, if less coherent than the Greek ideal, nevertheless antedated Plato by two centuries. All the great traditions teach moderation.

O GOD OF WISDOM, give us true wisdom to understand the middle path of moderation, lest we lose ourselves through the extremes of asceticism or lust. Grant us thy peace. Amen.

131　A LOOK AT LIFE

BUDDHISM

Birth is painful, old age is painful, sickness is painful, death is painful, sorrow, lamentation, dejection, and despair are painful. Contact with unpleasant things is painful, not getting what one wishes is painful.

(The cure of the pain is) the cessation without a remainder of that craving; abandonment, forsaking, release, non-attachment.

SAMYUTTA-NIKAYA 5.420

"Right views" meant, according to Buddha, understanding the painfulness involved in the very process of living. No one can go through life without first crying for his mother, then suffering injuries both physical and spiritual, growing old and dying, meanwhile meeting with situations involving frustration, sorrow, and despair. To understand the nature of life and to objectify its experiences—this leads to peace of mind and heart. We must not expect what life cannot offer.

Probably for most of us, life on the whole is not nearly so tragic as Buddha suggests. Yet sooner or later we all meet with situations in which resignation seems our only salvation.

GOD OF WISDOM, enter into our hearts, that we may learn the secret of contentment amid the frustrations of life. May we not yield to despair. Amen.

132   RIGHT INTENTION

NEW TESTAMENT

You have heard that it was said to the men of old, "You shall not kill; and whoever kills shall be liable to judgment." But I say to you that every one who is angry with his brother shall be liable to judgment. . . . So if you are offering your gift at the altar, and there remember that your brother has something against you, leave your gift there before the altar and go; first be reconciled to your brother, and then come and offer your gift.   MATTHEW 5:21-24

Prophets are men who have a way of judging people by their motives, not just by the outward act. Buddha, like Jesus, insisted on "right intention" as a qualification of the perfect life. Our motives, aims, and hopes are important. Many people are so thoughtless as not even to realize what their goals are. An effective life is conditioned by intelligent self-knowledge. We must understand what we are aiming at. The good life requires that we modify our goals in the light of a norm of good conduct. This requires much thought.

Basic is the insight that the good is the desirable and that

147

growth comes from the setting up of proper goals which are patiently sought.

O GOD, help us in the simple task of understanding ourselves and our aims in life, and may our goals be in harmony with thy will. Amen.

133 RIGHT SPEECH

BUDDHISM

Better than a thousand utterances composed of meaningless words is one sensible word on hearing which one becomes peaceful.
                                                      DHAMMAPADA 100
A man is not learned simply because he talks much. He who is tranquil, free from hatred, free from fear, he is said to be learned.
                                                      DHAMMAPADA 258
Guarding his speech, restraining well his mind, let a man not commit anything wrong with his body. He who keeps these three roads of action clear, will achieve the way taught by the wise.
                                                      DHAMMAPADA 281
The mendicant who controls his tongue, who speaks wisely, not (puffed up), who illuminates the meaning and the law, his utterance is sweet.   DHAMMAPADA 363

Our schools today place much stress upon effective communication, spoken and written. The Buddha regarded it as a moral duty to study to make our speech a clear vehicle of our thoughts. If we have right thoughts, we ought to communicate them to others. Certainly there is no proper place for lying, deceit, slander, and profanity in the good life. We can do untold harm by asserting untruths about our colleagues and acquaintances. Profanity reveals a lack of self-discipline. The final aim of speech should be like all our actions: to bring about a better world.

148

Rotary International has a "Four-Way Test" which we all might adopt:

1. Is it the truth?
2. Is it fair to all concerned?
3. Will it build good will and better friendships?
4. Will it be beneficial to all concerned?

O GOD, may all our speech show proper regard for the truth, with charity for others, and may we cultivate clear and forceful self-expression. Amen.

134   RIGHT ACTION

HINDUISM

Common men talk bagfuls of religion but act not a grain of it, while the wise man speaks little, but his whole life is a religion acted out.   RAMAKRISHNA

Mature religion requires more than good thoughts, good words, and good intentions. Behavior is the ultimate test. Said Confucius, "A gentleman is ashamed to let his words outrun his deeds." Jesus said, "You will know them by their fruits."

It is of course well to stress good motives and good words. But to mean well and do ill indicates something less than the best in the moral life.

O GOD, may we perform daily the deeds of kindness which we so easily praise. May we still, however, hold to ideals so lofty as to be a continual challenge to our powers. Amen.

For as in one body we have many members, and all members do not have the same function, so we, though many, are one body in Christ, and individually members one of another. Having gifts that differ according to the grace given to us, let us use them: if prophecy, in proportion to our faith; if service, in our serving; he who teaches, in his teaching; he who exhorts, in his exhortation; he who contributes, in liberality; he who gives aid, with zeal; he who does acts of mercy, with cheerfulness.

ROMANS 12:4-8

The variety of gifts which we share implies that one of us will do better in one type of position and another in another. The work of the world could not be carried on unless this were so. Whatever we take up as a means of earning a living—a "livelihood"—should be interpreted as a vocation to which we are called through divine guidance. To think of our work in this way would most likely transform it from animal rivalry to an opportunity for service. Some might even have to give up their customary livelihood by viewing it from this angle. For most vocations, however, the transformation can be made and should be made.

For the Buddha the greatest vocation was that of the monk, or, as we should say, of the ministry. But nearly all vocations may become a ministry when viewed in this light.

O GOD, help us to transform our vocations into channels of service, that we may be instruments of thy mercy. Amen.

Let love be genuine; hate what is evil, hold fast to what is good; love one another with brotherly affection; outdo one another in showing honor.

.   .   .   .

Bless those who persecute you; bless and do not curse them. Rejoice with those who rejoice, weep with those who weep. Live in harmony with one another; do not be haughty, but associate with the lowly; never be conceited. Repay no one evil for evil, but take thought for what is noble in the sight of all. If possible, so far as it depends upon you, live peaceably with all.

ROMANS 12:9-10, 14-18

Our lives depend on the direction in which we turn our attention. Those who are mindful of petty personal relationships will be petty, jealous, cruel, and vain. Those who turn their minds to the promotion of peace and happiness will themselves be happy and noble. They who wish to serve must be mindful of the sciences and human techniques through which to serve. Artists and scientists become such only by properly directing their total efforts and by concentrating upon details which in themselves might be unattractive. Only a disciplined and self-directed life will be rewarded with real success.

Right mindfulness means that our attention will be directed, not by external and accidental circumstances, but by an inner principle of justice, generosity, and contentment.

O GOD, may we continually direct our attention to the promotion of peace and happiness among men. May we never cease to study the means by which to serve. Amen.

These wise ones, meditative, persevering, always putting forth strenuous effort, attain to nirvana, the highest freedom and happiness.

If a person is reflective, if he rouses himself, if he is ever-mindful, if his deeds are pure, if he acts with consideration, if he is self-restrained and lives according to law, his glory will increase.

.   .   .   .

Give not yourselves over to sloth or to the intimacy with lust and sensual pleasures. He who meditates with earnestness attains great joy.   DHAMMAPADA 23-24, 27

Someone said, on hearing a great pianist play, "I would give anything to be able to play like that." The pianist kindly replied, "Would you give five hours a day for six days in the week throughout the year, with all your strength and all your heart?" To do anything well takes more than merely turning the mind to it. It takes much hard concentration to acquire the necessary technique; it calls for dedication of strength and heart, for patience and perseverance. If we dedicate ourselves to the twofold task of building a spiritual life within and helping others to live happily and well, that too will require much concentration —not just a thought now and then.

When people spend so little time concentrating on the problems of the good life, can we be surprised that the world is confused?

O GOD, purify our purposes and give us patience with strength, that we may accomplish the tasks of freedom and peace. Amen.

(Virtues) are not infused into us from without. . . . "Seek and you will find them. Neglect and you will lose them."

MENCIUS 6.1.6.7

From the Son of Heaven down to the mass of the people, all must consider the cultivation of the person the root of everything besides.

It cannot be, when the root is neglected, that what should spring from it will be well ordered.   THE GREAT LEARNING

There is a fundamental agreement among all traditions on the need for the fullest possible realization of human resources. Jesus came that we might have life and have it more abundantly. He taught that every person is a child of God and should be treated with respect for his intrinsic worth. For Hinduism the individual self in its deepest experiences is the reflection of the absolute Self. For Buddha everything is subordinate to the cultivation of the individual as suggested by the Eightfold Noble Path. Confucius laid great stress upon the fullest possible realization of human nature at its best—in the image of God, as we would say. Like Jefferson, Confucius had faith in the common man and believed that everyone should be educated. Like the great prophets in all traditions, he was a teacher, and his whole life was dedicated to the best that he could draw out of his pupils, whom he in turn inspired with the spirit of human service. The Greek tradition stresses self-realization. The human heritage is pre-eminently positive.

Clearly there are human resources for both good and evil. What is desired is the realization of the good.

153

GOD MAKE US HUMBLE AND DISCERNING, that without prejudice we may see the divine image in all men regardless of race, class, or nationality. May we spare no effort to realize the full image of God in ourselves and our associations. Amen.

139 RESPONSIBILITY OF THE SELF

BUDDHISM

Evil is done by self alone, by self alone is one stained; by self alone is evil left undone, by self alone one is purified. Purity and impurity depend on one's own self. No man can purify another.
DHAMMAPADA 165

Let no one neglect his own task for the sake of another's, however great; let him, after he has discerned his own task, devote himself to his task.
DHAMMAPADA 166

It is all too easy to get into the habit of blaming others for what happens to us or for what we fail to accomplish. But Buddhism teaches, as did Jeremiah, that each man is responsible for his own sin. What happens to us externally may seem important, but it is not nearly so important as what happens to us internally. No one has the power that the self has to control the experience of the inner spirit. Not even God can impose our ultimate choices, either good or bad, although some theologians argue to the contrary. Even good preachers or good teachers are limited in their influence on people.

In the final analysis all education is self-education, and all spiritual achievement is made through the struggles of

154

the self alone. This is not to deny that God and his ministers do help us.

O GOD, make us humble as we realize our own responsibility for the good or bad that passes through our souls. May we build the strength that comes with good choices. Amen.

140   THE BLISS OF GOODNESS

BUDDHISM

If a man commits sin, let him not do it again and again. Let him not set his heart on it. Sorrowful is the accumulation of evil conduct.

If a man does what is good, let him do it again and again. Let him set his heart on it. Happiness is the outcome of good conduct.

DHAMMAPADA 117-118

Writes Radhakrishnan, "These verses are an emphatic expression of the Buddhist principle that punishment comes from the moral order which reacts on those who break it. . . . The view that God intervenes in the world to make guilty people suffer is for the Buddha a sheer superstition." Gandhi put it thus: "Truth for me is God, and God's laws and God are not different things or facts, in the sense that an earthly king and his law are different." God does not arbitrarily punish or withhold punishment. Plato taught that goodness is inherently desirable, that it needs no reward outside of itself. The good life is the satisfying life; evil is at odds with itself and causes all sorts of suffering within and without. The good life is the harmonious and happy life. It brings eternal bliss.

We may conceive of God's mercy as an integral part of the divine law of human life, to be enjoyed happily by all who humbly realize their spiritual need.

O God, may we experience the real blissfulness of goodness, as truly as we desire the inspiration of beauty and the support of truth. Amen.

141 REWARDS OF REVERENCE

BUDDHISM

To him who constantly practises reverence and respects the aged, four things will increase, life (length of days), beauty, happiness, strength.

But he who lives a hundred years, wicked and unrestrained, a life of one day is better if a man is virtuous and reflecting.

DHAMMAPADA 109

The quality of life is far more important than the quantity, according to the Dhammapada. Clearly this passage aims to encourage the attitude of reverence and of respect for the aged. These are excellent virtues, although the rewards which are promised are not always realized. Length of life does not necessarily result from reverence and filial faithfulness, since we know that many reverent and kind people die untimely deaths. But happiness, inward strength, and even a kind of spiritual peace and beauty do flow from a life that is reverent and respectful toward the elders. In any case, good people are reverent; that is, deeply respectful, loving, and sincerely deferent to divine values. Good people also respect the aged. Young people are inclined to be thoughtless of the feelings of the aged, but growing maturity begets respect, honor, sympathy, and care.

Reverence and respect need not and should not be in conflict with progressive religious and social thinking.

O GOD, may we share with reverence the wisdom, love, and bliss which are the essence of thy being. Help us to console the aged and those who need our sympathy. Amen.

142 THE STRENGTH OF GOODNESS

CONFUCIANISM

To dwell in the wide house of the world, to stand in the correct seat of the world, and to walk in the great path of the world; when he obtains his desire for office, to practise his principles for the good of the people; and when that desire is disappointed, to practise them alone; to be above the power of riches and honors to make dissipated, of poverty and mean condition to make swerve from principle, and of power and force to make bend: these characteristics constitute the great man.

MENCIUS 3.2.2.3

Some have criticized Mencius for being too self-righteous in this passage. Certainly we find no sense of sin and little humility. Yet Mencius was a faithful follower of the humble Confucius, and in this passage he states dramatically his firm conviction that the great man is the good man. That is, he is one who in public office is truly concerned for the welfare of his people. Or if he is not fortunate enough to be a public servant, he will serve privately and without recognition just because it is good to do so. Neither wealth nor honor, poverty nor force can deflect the good—and great—man from the path of honor, justice, and service to his fellow man.

157

Surely if the moral life has any real status in the universe, we may then be confident that goodness and greatness are inseparable.

HEAVENLY FATHER, we would dedicate ourselves to the good, as thou art good. May we experience a renaissance of moral strength and greatness. Give us courage and patience as we struggle against pride and pettiness. Amen.

143   ORGANIZING GOODNESS

SHINTO

I. *The fundamental principles: Fidelity to vocation; an earnest desire to carry out the Way (of the Warrior; i.e. Bushido); efforts devoted to its practice.*

II. *Training of the mind; Composure of mind; Magnanimity; Purity of sentiment; Gentleness; Refinement, etc.*

III. *Training in virtues and the perfection of ability.*

IV. *Self-introspection and self-restraint.*

V. *Mindfulness of dignity and propriety; Self-respect and gravity; Vigilance in seeing and hearing, etc.*

VI. *Vigilance in daily life; Daily life and its surrounding; the use of wealth and its significance in life, etc.*

BUSHIDO

This passage represents the efforts of a teacher to inspire young members of the *samurai* or Japanese warrior caste to live noble lives worthy of their vocation. Faithfulness in one's vocation requires a careful evaluation of its aims and possibilities in the complex web of society. Each vocation calls for special aptitudes and preparation, as well as for certain qualities of character and deportment. Self-knowledge and self-direction are necessary to the greatest success in any vocation. One who does not have a fundamental respect for his vocation will never be very happy or successful. Judged by the standards here enunciated, there must have been many men of true nobility in the patriotic *samurai* caste. The suggestions made here might well be applied to almost any worthy vocation. We could all profit by vocational self-evaluation. After all, the only way to achieve great goodness is by making the most of our special situation in life.

With the rise of vocational guidance and its testing program, we should expect a more harmonious society and better adjusted individuals than in the past.

O GOD, make us aware of the potentialities for human service in our daily work. May we earnestly devote ourselves to it. Amen.

144 THE LABORATORY OF VIRTUE

CONFUCIANISM

If you cannot cause them to have what they love in their families, they will forthwith proceed to be guilty of crime.

SHU CHING 5.4.3.5

The home is the laboratory of all virtue. There we can visibly perceive the effects of our actions on others and feel the results of their behavior on us. In the home there is usually the requisite charity to tolerate one another's faults with mutual criticism. The larger family generally affords a better laboratory than one that is too small. In any case, in the intimacy of the home we learn easily what virtue means in a very concrete manner. In the light of such environmental education, it is easy to understand the Confucian doctrine enunciated in the brief passage quoted above. When we pass beyond the intimacy of the family to that of the community and world, we are in danger of forgetting how actions affect one another.

In prophetic religion there is no stranger. All men are brothers. The norms of family virtue must be applied universally.

HEAVENLY FATHER, may we treasure in our hearts what we love in our families and thus make of the world and our communities one great family under God. May we harbor no motives toward strangers that would not stand the scrutiny of family relationships. Amen.

145 THE GOOD WORKMAN

ANCIENT BABYLONIA

If a builder build a house for someone, and does not construct it properly, and the house which he built fall in and kill its owner, then that builder shall be put to death.

If it ruin goods, he shall make compensation for all that has been ruined, and inasmuch as he did not construct properly this house which he built and it fell, he shall re-erect the house from his own means.

If a shipbuilder build a boat for someone, and do not make it tight, if during that same year that boat is sent away and suffers injury, the shipbuilder shall take the boat apart and put it together tight at his own expense. HAMMURABI

The Babylonian Code of Hammurabi (early seventeenth century B.C.), from which this is taken, drew upon earlier Sumerian sources and in turn influenced later codes such as the Mosaic. Like the Mosaic Code, Hammurabi's reveals the ancient human commitment to the principles of strict justice. Punishment was often severe, calling for an eye for an eye, a life for a life. For example, if the physician operated on a patient and the patient died or was deformed, the physician's hand was to be cut off. Even the workman was held responsible for the integrity of his product. Our Pure Food and Drugs Acts illustrate how in our complex modern society we are trying to restore reasonable responsibility for our products. But much of that sort of responsibility cannot be legislated.

The all-too-human tendency is to demand justice for ourselves while neglecting to insure it for others.

God HELP US to be honorable and wholly responsible in all our business and professional relationships. May we not need to ask forgiveness for our failure to act justly. Amen.

146 WHO, ME?

CONFUCIANISM

King Hwuy of Leang said, "I wish quietly to receive your instructions."

Mencius replied, "Is there any difference between killing a man with a stick and with a sword?" The king said, "There is no difference." "Is there any difference between doing it with a sword and with the style of government?" "There is no difference," was the reply.   MENCIUS 1

"Thou art the man," was Nathan's way of telling David that he had sinned. Mencius apparently showed the same degree of courage with King Hwuy of Leang. He seems to

161

have survived the hazard about as well as Nathan did. Many a courageous soul has made a bitter enemy out of a friend by frank but benevolent criticism. Certainly we must weigh our friend's character before telling him his faults, for if we do more harm than good, it will not pay. Very few people can profit by an accusing finger unless that finger is one's own. Self-analysis through meditation, indeed, is one way of applying the technique of discovering our own faults. Or we might turn the situation about and request our most trusted friend or relative to tell us our faults. Let us be sure that we mean it, however. It is a human weakness to deal in generalities and to back down when "thou art the man."

Unusual caution and keen discretion are required of anyone who would try to bring about even the greatest of goods by interfering in the personal morality of his friends.

GOD GIVE US TACT AND CHARITY in our judgments of one another. May our courage be matched by our love and wisdom. Amen.

147 THE IMPORTANCE OF SELF

TAOISM

Our life is our own possession, and its benefit to us is very great. Regarding its dignity, even the honor of being Emperor could not compare with it. Regarding its safety, were we to lose it for one morning, we could never again bring it back.

LÜ-SHIH CH'UN-CH'IU

There is perhaps a danger that some, in their zeal for holiness, will go too far in their unselfishness. After all, the self is important, and no one is quite as responsible for its growth and happiness as the individual himself is. This was the insight which the early Taoists had. Complete unselfishness would logically mean self-destruction. "I am only one, but still I am one," as Edward Everett Hale said. The golden rule of Jesus and other prophets required that we regard others as highly as we regard ourselves, not more highly. Our first responsibility is to ourselves, and that means that we should seek to realize the highest possible degree of spiritual selfhood. Said an ancient writer, "Preserving life and maintaining what is genuine in it, not allowing things to entangle one's person; this is what (the Taoist) Yang Chu established."

Normally speaking, we are more likely to err in the direction of selfishness than of unselfishness.

O GOD, may we truly make our lives amount to the most that is possible for us, through insight into the real values of life. May we "to our own selves be true," that our spiritual foundations may be firm. Amen.

148 WHOM WE TRUST

TAOISM

> *In governing the world,*
> *Let rule entrusted be*
> *To him who treats his rank*
> *As if it were his soul;*
> *World sovereignty can be*
> *Committed to that man*
> *Who loves all people*
> *As he loves himself.*

TAO TÊ CHING 13

This is the final stanza of a poem from the Tao Tê Ching extolling the virtues of selflessness and contentment. It is the selfish person who is ambitious. He wants high rank whether he deserves it or not. Such a person is bound to be discontented, for he will always be jealous of his position, and he will suffer disappointments. The preceding stanza reads:

> What does it mean, to say
> That "rank, like self,
> Involves acute distress"?
> I suffer most because
> Of me and selfishness.
> If I were selfless, then
> What suffering would I bear?

He who is not motivated by vanity and ambition will regard his position objectively, as merely an opportunity to serve. He does his honest best and is contented.

GRACIOUS GOD, may we be worthy of whatever rank we have, treating it as a gift of heaven to be used, not for self, but for the service for which it is intended. Amen.

149 CHOOSE THIS DAY

OLD TESTAMENT

"Now therefore fear the Lord, and serve him in sincerity and in faithfulness; put away the gods which your fathers served beyond the River, and in Egypt, and serve the Lord. And if you be unwilling to serve the Lord, choose this day whom you will serve, whether the gods your fathers served in the region beyond the River, or the gods of the Amorites in whose land you dwell; but as for me and my house, we will serve the Lord."

.   .   .   .

And the people said to Joshua, "Nay; but we will serve the Lord." Then Joshua said to the people, "You are witnesses against yourselves that you have chosen the Lord, to serve him." . . . So Joshua made a covenant with the people that day.

JOSHUA 24:14-15, 21-22, 25

Israel had no idea of the vast importance of the choice which they were asked to make that day. Decisions would not be so hard if we knew all the consequences. Israel's choice would have been simple if they could have foreseen the growth of culture and the inadequacy of magic and polytheism in the light of modern knowledge. But the human situation is such that fateful choices must be made in the urgent present, before we find time to discover all relevant data. Man possesses a "dreadful freedom," as the existentialists put it. He *must* choose before he is ready. In such times the prophetic souls who spend much time in meditation have the great advantage, and mankind would do well to hearken. But this takes courage, as James Russell Lowell understood, for

Then to side with truth is noble when we share her wretched crust,
Ere her cause bring fame and profit, and 'tis prosperous to be just;
Then it is the brave man chooses, while the coward stands aside . . .
(Till) the multitude make virtue of the faith they had denied.

We cannot put off today's choices in our planetary community. They need far more meditation than we can possibly give them.

GOD HELP US in making right choices as we face a fearsome future. May we think with our hearts, minds, and souls, lest prejudice ensnare us to our destruction. Amen.

165

All within the Four Seas are . . . brothers.   ANALECTS 12.5

> *The people should be cherished,*
> *And not looked down upon.*
> *The people are the root of a country;*
> *The root firm, the country is tranquil.*
>
> SHU CHING 3.3.2

Whether or not the whole world is a brotherhood depends not on a biological fact so much as on the human heart. This is one area where "thinking makes it so." One man may limit brotherhood to his own family, class, or nationality. Another, hated or ridiculed by many, may truly be a brother to all. Edwin Markham expressed this situation forcefully in his famous quatrain:

> He drew a circle that shut me out—
> Heretic, rebel, a thing to flout.
> But love and I had the wit to win:
> We drew a circle that took him in.

It was a Chinese who drew the circle in the above-quoted scripture. The same circle has been drawn by Japanese, Iranians, Indians, Jews, and many others. Plain folks everywhere must realize the common humanity of all their fellow men, confident that mutual faith in each other is justified and that it will bring about a better world.

Much of the greatness of Jefferson and Lincoln lies in their trust in the good sense of common people.

O God, may we dedicate ourselves truly to the basic beliefs of democracy enunciated by all the great religions. We pray for the rise of the brotherhood of man, with peace and justice. Amen.

151 THE BONDS OF SYMPATHY

SHINTO

Nothing in all the world calls forth such gratitude as sincerity. Through oneness in sincerity the men of the four seas are brothers.

All men are brothers. All receive the blessings of the same heaven. The suffering of others is my suffering; the good of others is my good. TEXTS OF KUROZUMI KYO

"Sincerity" might be paraphrased as "that human quality of genuineness that creates a bond of sympathy." The great significance of the scripture passage is that it comes from Shinto, which is perhaps the most primitive of the great religions in modern times. The vision of universal brotherhood is confined to no time or place. It is an insight of the sincere heart. The fact is that the perception of the universal in the human heart is truly the vision of God, whose image all men bear in some degree. To share heaven's blessings—even to share human suffering—this is to share God. We can find God "even in the least of these," God's children.

In the light of the divine image in men, it is easy to see the sinfulness of hate, envy, and ill will.

God give us human sympathy and sincere appreciation of the worth of those who differ from us physically or culturally. Amen.

Even those who belong to the lower castes—women, Vaishyas, and Sudras too—can reach the highest spiritual realization, if they will take refuge in me. Need I tell you, then, that this is also true of the holy Brahmins and pious philosopher-kings? . . . Fill your heart and mind with me, adore me, make all your acts an offering to me, bow down to me in self-surrender. If you set your heart upon me thus, and take me for your ideal above all others, you will come into my Being. BHAGAVAD-GITA 9.32, 33

Human beings are alike in that they all face the basic insecurities of health, happiness, success in their work, and life itself. All need the insights of spiritual values and God's saving grace and consolation in times of sorrow. Such blessings of religion should be denied to no one. In the Hindu tradition, the Bhagavad-Gita rejects the sacredness of caste and offers God's saving grace to all. Vaishyas form the merchant caste; Sudras are workers. This passage promises that any who take refuge in Krishna will attain the highest spiritual goals.

The personal relationship with the divine, in Hinduism as in Christianity, is an added inspiration to spiritual realization.

O GOD, we would know thee as friend knows friend and have all men know thee in the unity of the spirit. Amen.

Not by birth does one become an outcaste, not by birth does one become a Brahmin; by deeds one becomes an outcaste, by deeds does one become a Brahmin.　　　VASALASUTTA 21

Him I call a Brahmin who does not hurt by body, speech, or mind, who is controlled in these three things.　　DHAMMAPADA 291

Him I call a Brahmin who, though he has committed no offence, bears patiently reproach, ill-treatment, imprisonment; who has endurance for his force and strength for his army.

DHAMMAPADA 399

Him I call a Brahmin who is without hostility among those who are hostile, who is peaceful among those with uplifted staves, who is unattached among those who are attached.

DHAMMAPADA 406

Even more radically than the Gita, Buddha aimed at the reformation of Hinduism, especially its caste system. An outcaste was at the bottom of the social scale in India, while a Brahmin—a priest—was at the top. According to the system, everyone was born into his socioeconomic class. Buddha perceived that this was not just. A man's native ability and his achievements in life should determine his rank in society. The ferment in India today shows a trend toward the Buddhist ideal. Other lands are witnessing the struggle against caste.

While the standard by which to judge excellence is not specifically stated in the quoted scriptures, by implication it is good will, service, and related virtues.

O GOD, help us to judge people not by their social or economic status, but by their character and human achievements. May we judge ourselves by that same standard. Amen.

> *To take all you want*
> *Is never as good*
> *As to stop when you should.*
> *Scheme and be sharp*
> *And you'll not keep it long.*
> *One never can guard*
> *His home when it's full*
> *Of jade and fine gold. . . .*

TAO TÊ CHING 9

Temperance seems to be the main theme of these lines. The virtue is examined from the point of view of self-interest. Lao Tzu is saying that the virtuous life is really the most desirable life. We are not missing a lot of fun by being temperate. The selfish, scheming, conniving individual only makes enemies and ends by eating his cake in a corner—or perhaps he is surrounded by insincere, scheming sycophants who have no more use for him than he has for them. Down deep is fear—fear of losing his dishonest gains and fear of betrayal. Nor does he enjoy a good conscience. It really is good to be temperate, generous, and kind.

Plato hints that many good people are disturbed by the suspicion that somehow they may be missing the pleasures of sin. Perhaps such people lack the virtue of real faith in goodness, wisdom, and understanding.

O GOD, may goodness and mercy follow us all the days of our lives, that we may dwell in the divine presence forever. Amen.

I do not know how a man without truthfulness is to get on. How can a large carriage be made to go without the crossbar?
ANALECTS 2.22

Truthfulness is no small virtue. It is so large that few people can attain it even though they may never tell a lie. Normally we use verbal symbols as a medium through which to convey the truth. By persistent effort we may cultivate the ability to use words as an effective means of revealing the truth as we know it. The petty person who deceives by intent moves farther and farther away from the ideal of truthfulness. One who exercises all the powers of his mind and heart comes closer and closer to it throughout a lifetime. Certainly one will neither understand others nor be understood by them unless he fixes his mind faithfully on truthfulness, which is the foundation of personal and social integrity, as Confucius perceived.

People of good will may withhold a truth if it is likely to do more harm than good. In principle, however, truthfulness is the ideal.

> Holy Spirit, Truth divine,
> Dawn upon this soul of mine;
> Word of God, and inward Light,
> Wake my spirit, clear my sight.   Amen.

The gentleman does not mind not being in office; all he minds about is whether he has qualities that entitle him to office. He does not mind failing to get recognition; he is too busy doing the things that entitle him to recognition.   ANALECTS 4.14

We are impressed with the great concern of Confucius for the cultivation of human virtues. Confucius shows penetrating insight into moral values and personal worth. Nothing short of perfection would satisfy. And that perfection involved both the outward act and the inward motive. His insistence in this particular passage is that the great man does not seek office, but that he does possess the qualities which would make him a good public official. Confucius was never given public recognition in his lifetime; few great men, especially prophets, have been. But that is not the important consideration for the great man, since goodness is its own reward. There are always some—like Confucius' own disciples—who understand and appreciate the true values of the spirit.

No doubt great men have suffered through being misunderstood and unappreciated. Yet they must have felt the deep consolation of their own integrity.

O GOD, may we always be more concerned with our own fitness than with recognition by others. Put greatness into our hearts, that we may live worthy of our responsibilities. Amen.

Tzu-kung said, The faults of a gentleman are like eclipses of the sun or moon. If he does wrong, everyone sees it. When he corrects his fault, every gaze is turned up towards him.   ANALECTS 19.21

Confucianism never gets any closer to a sense of sin than in this passage. Here we find no upheaval of the soul, no awareness of a holy presence whose perfection accentuates the feeling of sinfulness. Yet there is the common-sense recognition of man's proneness to do wrong and of the need for humility in acknowledging the error and correcting it. There is a certain nobility, says Tzu-kung, in correcting one's fault. People do not expect great men to have faults. But when they do and when they discover and correct them, then people look up to them as they do to the sun or moon coming out of an eclipse. It is not really a thing to be wondered at that great men should at times find themselves in error, for all men are human. Greatness consists in finding the error and humbly correcting it.

It has been suggested that if the practical results are identical, the Confucian doctrine of the nobility of correcting error is the same as the Christian doctrine of repentance.

O GOD OF PURITY, help us to recognize our sins in the light of thy perfection and to repent with all our heart. Amen.

If a man were to conquer in battle a thousand times a thousand men, and another conquer one, himself, he indeed is the greatest of conquerors.   DHAMMAPADA 103

Here is a thought found in the literature of many cultures. It points out the difficulty of self-conquest, of the rule of man's better judgment over his passions and impulses. Self-conquest means self-control, temperance, resulting in a mode of behavior which has been wisely planned. Some men are unable to control their appetites for harmful food or drink. Others fail to control the passions of their sensuous nature. Still others simply fail to conquer their laziness and thereby fail to realize greatness. Life can be beautiful if we first conquer ourselves and then follow in the path of wisdom. Self-control is an ideal of Christianity as of all other great religions.

For each person the problem is unique. Each must find the clue to his own weakness and plan deliberate strategy to overcome it.

O GOD, we would know the way of wisdom and rule our lives thereby. May we face frankly the difficulty of self-conquest and find the greater satisfaction in ruling ourselves. Amen.

SHINTO

God is the Great Parent of your real self. . . .

Do not bring bitterness to your own heart by anger at the things that are past.

Do not profess love with your lips while you harbor hatred in your heart.

One should not be mindful of suffering in his own life and un-mindful of suffering in the lives of others. KONKO KYO

Beautiful qualities of the soul are revealed in this text from a Shinto sect. It is perceived that the true self is a child of God. We reflect God's image only when we achieve our soul's integrity. There is no bitterness in God—only the greatest benevolence—and it is sheer folly for one in his image to be angry over things that are past and can no longer be changed. Not even God can turn back the wheels of time, though he is not pleased with the events of history. Nor is there hypocrisy in God. No merit for us is gained by speaking words of love while hating with our hearts. Deepest of all is the divine compassion for those who suffer. As we long for comfort in our suffering, so let us be God's comforting angels through compassion for others.

It has been suggested that salvation consists in achieving the complete integrity or wholeness of the soul. A single decision sometimes changes a whole life by giving it a unifying principle.

O PERFECT LOVE, may we think on thee daily and fix thy pure image in our souls. Amen.

For freedom Christ has set us free; stand fast therefore, and do not submit again to a yoke of slavery.

.   .   .   .

For you were called to freedom, brethren; only do not use your freedom as an opportunity for the flesh, but through love be servants of one another. For the whole law is fulfilled in one word, "You shall love your neighbor as yourself." But if you bite and devour one another take heed that you are not consumed by one another.

.   .   .   .

Now the works of the flesh are plain: immorality, impurity, licentiousness, idolatry, sorcery, enmity, strife, jealousy, anger, selfishness, dissension, party spirit, envy, drunkenness, carousing, and the like. I warn you, as I warned you before, that those who do such things shall not inherit the kingdom of God. But the fruit of the Spirit is love, joy, peace, patience, kindness, goodness, faithfulness, gentleness, self-control; against such there is no law.

GALATIANS 5:1, 13-15, 19-23

Christian freedom is freedom worthy of sons of God. (Galatians 4:6-7) In order to educate the primitive-minded Galatians, Paul tried to illustrate what it meant to be children of God, free as he was but still bound by the laws of his own nature. This principle ruled out all immorality, impurity, superstition, intemperance, and ill will. It entailed the qualities of the Spirit. Among these qualities love is primary. Joy and peace also belong to the divine life in man—not sadness, not strife. Good will and self-direction in their various forms constitute the remaining list of the Spirit's fruit. The list deserves our prayerful contemplation.

The spiritual life is not mysterious and otherworldly. It is a life that thrives on the works of the spirit.

SPIRIT OF GOD, dwell in our hearts, that we may ever reveal thy love, joy, peace, kindness, goodness, faithfulness, gentleness, and self-control. Amen.

161 WHEN NOT TO ARGUE

HINDUISM

Dispute not. As you rest firmly on your own faith and opinion allow others also the equal liberty to stand by their own faiths and opinions. By mere disputation you will never succeed in convincing another of his error. When the grace of God descends on him, each one will understand his own mistakes. RAMAKRISHNA

When people argue, the assumption is that there is only one truth on any given issue and that reason should establish what that truth is. Then all intelligent people would accept it. Unfortunately it does not work this way. Experience is very complex, and each person has different experiences. Prejudices are many and deep. People often believe essentially what they want to believe anyway. Only when two or more persons come together to exchange experiences and insights in the spirit of discovery is reasoning effective. Otherwise it is of little use to argue. You may even make an enemy. "Mere disputation" will never succeed, although there are more subtle ways of breaking down prejudice and leading good people to a larger view of life.

Good will is even more essential than logic in arriving at a common understanding.

GOD OF TRUTH, may we be tolerant of good people who differ with us and seek ever more effectively to keep open our own minds and hearts. Amen.

162 SUBTLE PREJUDICE

When you hear words that are distasteful to your mind, you must inquire whether they be not right; when you hear words that accord with your own views, you must inquire whether they be not contrary to what is right.   SHU CHING 4.5.2.2

When we become aware of the subtle nature of prejudice, then we are in a position to destroy it in at least one case, namely, our own. This can be done by following the advice given by the Confucian scripture above. In terms of contemporary culture, there are innumerable opportunities for good people to inquire into ways of thinking different from their own customary ways. The almost universal tendency is for people to read the kind of literature or listen to the kind of speaking that will strengthen their present beliefs. Lest they be overlooking something important through the deceit of prejudice, they would do well to inquire into other points of view.

Truth is truth, from whatever religion or culture it may come. And truth is good.

GOD, GIVE US COURAGE to discover new truth. May we love the truth as we love thee, since truth is one with thy essence. Amen.

*Let there be no compulsion in religion. Now is the right way
made distinct from error. . . .*

*God is the patron of believers; he bringeth them out of dark-
ness into light.*   KORAN 2:257-258

*To every one have we given a law and a way. . . . And if God
had pleased, he would have made you all (all mankind) one
people (people of one religion). But he hath done otherwise, that
he might try you in that which he hath severally given unto you:
wherefore press forward in good works. Unto God shall ye return,
and he will tell you that concerning which we disagree.*

KORAN 5:48

To you your religion, and to me my religion.   KORAN 109:6

No doubt we will have to forgive those who are so utterly convinced of the rightness of their beliefs that they
must try to convert everyone else to the same way of thinking. Islam has gained a reputation for such intolerance,
and yet we find Muhammad teaching in these passages the
full freedom of faith. Perhaps Christians have not made
enough effort to understand and appreciate the real Islam.
In this case, at any rate, we can all learn from Muhammad
the lesson of charity in matters of faith.

It has been said that when we get to heaven, we may be
surprised at the people who are there.

GOD GIVE US FAITH without intolerance; give us charity
without the loss of our own spiritual integrity. Amen.

Moreover, the Jews say, "The Christians lean on nought"; "On nought lean the Jews," say the Christians: Yet both are readers of the Book. So with like words say they who have no knowledge. But on the resurrection day, God shall judge between them as to that in which they have differed. . . . KORAN 2:107

Then we caused our apostles to follow in their footsteps; and we caused Jesus the son of Mary to follow them; and we gave him the Evangel, and we put into the hearts of those who followed him kindness and compassion; but as to the monastic life, they invented it themselves. . . .

God is Forgiving, Merciful; that the people of the Book may know that they have no control over aught of the favors of God, and that these gifts of grace are in the hands of God, who vouchsafeth them to whom he will; for God is of immense bounty.

KORAN 57:27-29

A fault of many earnest people is that they try to play the part of God. They know who is going to be saved and who is going to be damned. They know exactly what everybody ought to believe. They know what everyone should do, and they try to make them do it. When dear friends and family differ with them, they worry themselves sick because God's will is not being done. How can they be so sure that they know what is God's will for everyone? This tendency to be sure of one's own judgment leads to sectarianism in religion. Paul warned against sects. Jesus prayed that his followers might all be one and recognized faithful disciples who were "not of this fold." The great prophets are not sectarian.

180

An open mind need not be a mind without its own conviction.

O GOD, may a great sympathy enlarge our own faith,
that we may commune with thy people everywhere without
losing sight of the values of our own traditions. Amen.

165 THE UNITY OF RELIGION

SIKHISM

There is no Hindu, nor is there a Muslim.

GRANTH

Nanak, founder of Sikhism, spoke these words revealing
his deep conviction that all religions are essentially one.
There may be a variety of names by which people call God,
but there is only one God to whom those names refer. Some
may be ignorant of the true nature of that God and may
be superstitious about myth and magic, but all earnest
people seek their spiritual salvation. Nanak was especially
bothered about the antagonism of Hindu and Muslim and
tried to get both to realize their essential unity. Fellowship
across the frontiers of faith seems the least that we can
practice in view of the human-heartedness and true sincerity of the followers of those various faiths.

Not all representatives of any faith are perfect. If we
could know a few of the best in other faiths, our souls
would be enriched.

O GOD OF MANY NAMES, may we be as universal in our
sympathies as art thou, who sendest thy rain upon the
just and the unjust and carest for our enemies as surely as
for our friends. Amen.

As one and the same material, water, is called by different names by different peoples, one calling it water, another eau, a third aqua, and another pani, so the one Sat-chit-ananda, the everlasting-intelligent-bliss, is invoked by some as God, by some as Allah, by some as Jehovah, by some as Hari, and by others as Brahman. RAMAKRISHNA

Here is the witness of another prophet to the essential unity of all religions, through which God tries to speak to man. His point is good—that it matters not by what name God is called; he is still the same, the one and only God. But it matters much how men conceive of God. As Emerson said, it is only

> When half-gods go,
> The gods arrive.

John Addington Symonds affirmed a similar sentiment:

> Gods fade; but God abides and in man's heart
> Speaks with the clear unconquerable cry
> Of energies and hopes that cannot die.

It would be flaccid to maintain that all ideas of God are of equal value. Even those who belong to a great prophetic tradition often fail to comprehend their heritage.

Let us not be too sure that just because another calls his God Allah or Brahman, he does not know the true God as well as we.

O GOD, live thou within our hearts, by whatever name. Give us the grace and spirit to witness to thy presence. Amen.

As rain does not break through a well-thatched house, so passion does not make its way into a reflecting mind.

DHAMMAPADA 14

Thoughtfulness is like a good roof in the structure of a man's life. So said the Buddha, or some unknown disciple who was inspired by him. Rain is the passionate element which it is desirable to keep out. A human being who acts on impulse and passion is unworthy of his human nature. Thoughtfulness can save a man much sorrow and regret. As Aristotle said, man differs from the animals by virtue of his rationality. By rational self-control he becomes humanly mature. How many of us allow passion and impulse to rule our lives? How many cultivate reflection? The thoughtful life does need cultivation by means of the reading of good books and the forming of regular habits of meditation.

A list of the books that we have read during the past year might indicate how much—or little—we value wisdom.

GOD GIVE US the wisdom to organize our time for the earnest pursuit of truth and understanding. Amen.

As a solid rock is not shaken by a strong gale, so wise men are not moved amidst blame and praise.

Even as a deep lake is clear and calm so also wise men become tranquil after they have listened to the laws. DHAMMAPADA 81-82

The solid strength of a rock is likened to the wisdom of a man. Neither the wise man nor the solid rock is easily moved by external forces. The unwise are easily affected by the fortunes of life and by the wills of other people. The simplest means of moving most people is by flattery, praise, or censure. People like the approval of their fellows. The unwise are greatly influenced by censure or praise. But the wise man directs his life by an inner principle. He knows what his essential goals are, and his behavior is always relative to them and therefore steadfast.

The approval of our fellow men is generally desirable. It should not, however, be the primary motivating force in our lives.

GOD GRANT US the strength that comes from inward harmony and steadfast, worthy goals. Amen.

By letting go, it all gets done;
The world is won by those who let it go!
But when you try and try,
The world is then beyond the winning.

TAO TÊ CHING 48

The world may be known
Without leaving the house. . . .
The further you go,
The less you will know.

TAO TÊ CHING 47

Many of the things over which we fret and sweat could just as well be neglected. There is too much striving in the world, while the simple joys of life go unattended. Wordsworth wrote truly:

The world is too much with us; late and soon,
Getting and spending, we lay waste our powers:
Little we see in Nature that is ours;
We have given our hearts away, a sordid boon!

There are many who rove about the earth without seeing much that means anything to them, while others, like Immanuel Kant, sit at home and become informed about all things.

The world within is not an empty world, but it needs special cultivation from within.

Teach me, Father, how to go
Softly as the grasses grow;

Hush my soul to meet the shock
Of the wild world as a rock;
But my spirit, propped with power,
Make as simple as a flower.   Amen.

170   SOULS WORTHY OF ETERNITY

HINDUISM

Those whose conduct has been good will quickly attain some good birth, the birth of a Brahmin, a Kshatriya, or a Vaishya. But those whose conduct is evil will quickly attain an evil birth, the birth of a dog, or a hog, or a candala.

CHANDOGYA UPANISHAD 5.10.7

The Hindu doctrine of reincarnation takes a variety of forms. Understood literally, as probably few enlightened Hindus would do, the doctrine has little value. As a myth, it teaches personal responsibility for our decisions and actions in this life and encourages a reverence for all life, since even the animals are said to embody the departed souls of friends or relatives. Rebirth as a Brahmin—the highest caste, the priestly—was regarded as the greatest reward. Kshatriyas were soldiers or rulers, and Vaishyas were artisans and entrepreneurs. The Hindu doctrine of rewards and punishments in the next life is intended to promote faithfulness and kindness in the present life.

There is a tendency today to take a new look at mythology, which may imaginatively embody our deepest aspirations and needs.

O GOD, help us to feel thy eternal presence in our lives, and may we live so as to be worthy of eternity. Amen.

Killing (animals) he thinks good sport, and derives mirth from it:

Away with that fool's company, he increases his own unright-eousness. AKARANGA SUTRA 1.3.2.3

Jainism's doctrine of noninjury is comparable with Schweitzer's "reverence for life," except that Jainism carries its doctrine to absurd extremes. The motive is somewhat different also. In principle, however, it seems sound to regard all life as sacred and to deny the will to live only when an individual or species constitutes a threat to the values of higher organisms. Even when an animal species serves primarily as food supply for man, unnecessary cruelty is wicked. The sportsman who kills just for the "pleasure" of killing ought to be psychoanalyzed.

The sympathetic enjoyment of lower forms of life opens large areas for human exploration. It may reveal God to us.

O GOD, may we be sensitive to the divine kinship of all living things. Save us from cruelty. Amen.

Go ye now . . . and wander, for the gain of the many, for the welfare of the many, out of compassion for the world, for the good, for the gain, and for the welfare of gods and men.

MAHAVAGGA 1.11

This was the Buddha's great commission to his first disciples. Having learned the nature of the good life, he taught it to his disciples. Having taught it to his disciples, he then commanded them to go out and tell others. It is the old story of how one who has experienced great joy wishes to share it with the whole world. His great joy lay in the knowledge that happiness is the result neither of a life of pleasures nor of a life of ascetic self-denial, but of moderation, philosophic enlightenment, and the practice of simple virtues.

The Buddha's message seems worthy of a missionary enterprise. The fact is that most of the great religions teach his essential message of moderation and the peaceful life.

O GOD OF OUR SALVATION, may our joy in the knowledge of the life of the spirit be such that we must share it with all. Amen

CONFUCIANISM

O great teacher, thy virtue surpasses that of a thousand sages,
And thy way excels that of a hundred kings.
Rivaling the sun and moon,
Thy light shines forever.
Truly there is none
Like thee among us.

RITUAL PRAYER TO CONFUCIUS, MANCHU

A teacher and precepts are the most important treasures a man can have; to be without a teacher and precepts is the greatest of misfortunes.
HSUN-TZU

All of us have had teachers. We remember some of them with special gratitude. Society should reward its teachers more than it does, but the supreme reward of teaching lies in the influence which goes on and on. Only the greatest of teachers have set endless waves of influence moving. Confucius, Lao Tzu, Buddha, Zoroaster, Socrates, Hillel, Jesus, Muhammad, and Nanak are among the greatest. Gratitude to our teachers may appropriately be expressed through deeds done in their spirit. We owe a special debt to teachers in our church schools who serve faithfully and freely. The greatest of these seek first to be well informed lest they set in motion such influence as needs to be corrected.

The greatest honor to any teacher should be the practice of his precepts.

O GOD, give us great teachers, and help us to recognize them when they appear. May we never refuse to teach when our talents match the need. Amen.

The third (disposition) is not to beat your teacher with a snatched-up stick, and not to bring scandal upon his name, for the sake of annoying him, by uttering that which was not heard from your own teacher.

The fourth is that whatever is taught liberally by your own teacher you have to deliver back to the worthy. . . .

The ninth is to fully understand the forward movement of the religion . . . and to seek your share of the duty therein. . . .

ZAD-SPARAM 24

Teaching has had an immense influence on the progress of mankind. From such primitive beginnings as are implied in the third disposition quoted above, teaching has grown to become a respected and mighty profession. Think what an influence the daily teaching of science in our classrooms has had over the past century in America. Every child now looks at nature scientifically. If the great religious traditions—all of them without prejudice—could be taught daily, think what spiritual progress man might make. We need it to balance a science which may be all too successful without religion to match it.

Zoroaster (or a disciple) taught that there should be progress in religion. It would be bad for religion—and man—if there were not such growth.

GOD HELP US to grow in our religious understanding as in all else. May we seek truly to understand the message of the great teachers of mankind, and to share the message in our lives. Amen.

190

175 SPIRITUAL FORESIGHT

He also said to the multitudes, "When you see a cloud rising in the west, you say at once, 'A shower is coming'; and so it happens. And when you see the south wind blowing, you say, 'There will be scorching heat'; and it happens. You hypocrites! You know how to interpret the appearance of the earth and sky; but why do you not know how to interpret the present time?"

LUKE 12:54-56

Jesus was here scolding his hearers for not recognizing the kingdom of God when it was in their presence. Had they understood, they would have acted in a more significant way regarding its Messiah. We too fail to recognize and receive great teachers when we have them near at hand. And we fail to understand the trends of history as great events take place. Now the atomic age requires one world in order to survive. For more subtle reasons, we have long needed to build a united world civilization, but have failed even to try. Many are simply blind to the signs of the times, which today are multiplying and glaring at us ominously.

There are, of course, some encouraging signs. But there is no cause for complacency.

GOD HELP US to think clearly and perceive deeply in these times when greatness is an absolute necessity. May we be willing to relate our individual and community needs to the total world situation. Amen.

Pray then like this:

> *Our Father who art in heaven,*
> *Hallowed be thy name.*
> *Thy kingdom come,*
> *Thy will be done,*
>   *On earth as it is in heaven.*
> *Give us this day our daily bread;*
> *And forgive us our debts,*
>   *As we also have forgiven our debtors;*
> *And lead us not into temptation,*
>   *But deliver us from evil.*

For if you forgive men their trespasses, your heavenly Father also will forgive you; but if you do not forgive men their trespasses, neither will your Father forgive your trespasses.

MATTHEW 6:9-15

Even today the questions are significant: What really is prayer? Why should we pray? Surely it is not a form of magic to which we should resort instead of to technology when we want something. Prayer is primarily a spiritual experience, available to us at all times, whereby we may utilize the largely untapped spiritual resources of the universe. Through spiritual vitality we may even make changes in the physical universe, as Tennyson intimated:

> More things are wrought by prayer
> Than this world dreams of.

Tennyson, like many other poets, also perceived the spiritual nature of prayer:

> Thrice blest whose lives are faithful prayers,
>> Whose loves in higher love endure;

Jesus stressed the practical nature of the spirit's longings, suggesting that we pray for bread as well as for the kingdom of heaven. Truly we need both.

HEAVENLY FATHER, teach us to pray, that we may not neglect acquaintance with the spiritual reality of the universe. May our concern for the kingdom move us continually to prayerful effort, with actions that match our petitions. Amen.

177   THE MAKING OF GODS

SHINTO

Both heaven and hell come from one's own heart. Oh the sadness of wandering in the devil's prayers.

If in one's heart one is a kami, then one becomes a kami; if in one's heart one is a Buddha, then one becomes a Buddha; if in one's heart one is a serpent, then one becomes a serpent.

TEXTS OF KUROZUMI KYO

There is much imagination in this text of sectarian Shinto. Its author saw that heaven and hell are experiences of our own souls here and now. "Wandering in the devil's prayers" is the failure to direct ourselves in well-chosen paths. Aimless wandering is just what the devil wants us to do, for then he can catch us off guard and suggest intriguing acts of evil. "Kami" is the mysterious power which the Japanese believed to be divine. Kurozumi thought that kami could be captured in the heart, like any other great ideal. Everyman's god is whatever he puts first in his life. For some, god is fame or popularity; for others, god is money or political power. For still others, God is the perfection revealed by some great prophet.

Truly understood, there are more polytheists in the world than we are accustomed to think, in this enlightened age.

O GOD, we worship thee.

> Light being no blindness,
> Love no unkindness,
> Knowledge no ruin,
> Fear no undoing!
> From the cradle to the grave,—
> Save, O Save! Amen.

178   DISCERNMENT

OLD TESTAMENT

And God said to [Solomon], "Because you have asked this, and have not asked for yourself long life or riches or the life of your enemies, but have asked for yourself understanding to discern what is right, behold, I now do according to your word. Behold, I give you a wise and discerning mind, so that none like you shall arise after you. I give you also what you have not asked, both riches and honor, so that no other king shall compare with you, all your days. And if you will walk in my ways, keeping my statutes and my commandments, as your father David walked, then I will lengthen your days."   1 KINGS 3:11-14

This is a great story. Solomon in his dream chose wisdom rather than riches, honor, or long life; and God was then pleased to give him, with wisdom, all other good things.

The moral, of course, is that wisdom is the basis of all else; one who has wisdom will also get wealth and honor. This causal chain, taken literally, may be doubted. Yet wisdom is an intrinsic good and is worth all that it takes to get it. It comes slowly, with much patience and experience.

> Knowledge comes, but wisdom lingers,

as Tennyson understood. Santayana had this idea in mind when he composed his famous quatrain:

> O World, thou choosest not the better part!
> It is not wisdom to be only wise,
> And on the inward vision close the eyes,
> But it is wisdom to believe the heart.

Wisdom and good will can never be at odds.

> God give us wisdom, above all else.
> But make us work for it,
> Nor ever be discouraged
> In the search for it. Amen.

179 ORDER AND GROWTH

CONFUCIANISM

The ancients who wished to . . . order well their states . . . first regulated their families. Wishing to regulate their families, they first cultivated their persons. Wishing to cultivate their persons, they first rectified their hearts. Wishing to rectify their hearts, they first sought to be sincere in their thoughts. Wishing to be sincere in their thoughts, they first extended to the utmost their knowledge.   THE GREAT LEARNING

What logic in this Confucian scripture! No one can truly understand the problems of a state or community without understanding first the problems of his own family. Nor can he understand his family unless he understands himself. The key to self-understanding is a knowledge of one's own aims and motives—a knowledge of the heart. If we sincerely try to order our own personal lives by the fundamental principles of ethics, then we can begin to measure the conduct of others, beginning with our own family and friends. If goodness and harmony are a genuine and inseparable pair, then the good life may result for all, beginning with right hearts and wide and sincere knowledge. Certainly the good life requires the utmost extension of knowledge.

Philosophy should have a larger share than it does in modern education—the thinking through of the fundamental issues of life and conduct.

GOD HELP US to grow upon firm foundations of personal integrity and social benevolence. May we have true knowledge of ourselves and feel the divine inspiration to expand always in wisdom and good influence. Amen.

> *Do not try to cultivate fields too large;—*
> *The weeds will only grow luxuriantly.*
> *Do not think of winning people far away;—*
> *Your toiling heart will be grieved.*

SHIH CHING

Things have their root and their branches. Affairs have their end and their beginning. To know what is first and what is last will lead near to what is taught in the Great Learning.

THE GREAT LEARNING

The trouble with most of us is that we are too impatient—too unwilling to start at the beginning and cultivate first a field no larger than our powers permit. No one became a great musician without first learning the scales and practicing the techniques day after day and year after year. Whatever our ambitions may be, we must begin humbly and work long and hard, building patiently the strong foundation for greatness. Success depends to a large extent on knowing what is first and what comes next. It depends as much on work as on talent. Buffon is reported to have said, "Genius is nothing but a great aptitude for patience." Carlyle characterized genius as a "transcendent capacity of taking trouble."

Much of our discouragement can be cured by a generous mixture of honest self-appraisal and effort.

O GOD, may we discern our goals in the light of sound knowledge and then have the humility to begin at the beginning. Amen.

Mencius, another day, saw king Hwuy of Leang. The king went and stood with him by a pond, and, looking round at the large geese and deer, said, "Do wise and good princes also find pleasure in these things?"

Mencius replied, "Being wise and good, they have pleasure in these things. If they are not wise and good, though they have these things, they do not find pleasure." MENCIUS 1

Stated simply, this means that joy comes from within the man, not from without. It means that only the wise and good are truly happy. We sometimes envy those who have everything to make them happy: rich people, society's pace-setters, leaders of the state, and executives of industry. Yet we may be unaware of the unhappiness of many of these very persons. Someone recently said, "Money doesn't bring you happiness, but it enables you to buy a high-powered car to go in search of it." This assertion was supposed to squelch all opposition. But it was far from the real point. Unless one first has wisdom for making discriminating choices and character formed by kindly motives, happiness will still elude.

We may note that there is no intrinsic evil in wealth or power. Still, there is no joy in them alone.

O GOD, may we find satisfaction in doing our daily work for the joy of service. May we find divine fellowship therein. Amen.

From the want of benevolence and the want of wisdom will ensue the entire absence of propriety and righteousness. . . .
The man who would be benevolent is like the archer. The archer adjusts himself and then he shoots. If he misses, he does not murmur against those who surpass him. He simply turns round and seeks the cause of his failure in himself. MENCIUS 2

Here is the great combination of virtue: benevolence and wisdom. Benevolence is simply another word for love. Literally it means "well wishing," or "good-willing." Wisdom and love working together in the human personality are the foundation of all moral perfection and greatness. Archery was the main sport in ancient China. Any sport would illustrate just as well. When a competitor excels us, we do not censure him, but examine our own techniques instead. Self-knowledge is an essential part of wisdom.

With a little effort, anyone may secure the aid of competent counselors, having personality and aptitude tests. It is never too late—or too early—to take some of these tests for a better understanding of ourselves and our talents.

GOD MAKE US humble enough to realize our need of wisdom and wise enough to see the steps that we must take to achieve it. May we be ready to adjust ourselves benevolently to the realities of life. Amen.

199

The time to take care is before it is done.
Establish order before confusion sets in.
Tree trunks around which you can reach with your arms were at
first only miniscule sprouts.
A nine-storied terrace began with a clod.

TAO TÊ CHING 64

The world is a pretty sick place, and we can do something about it by proper diagnosis and treatment. Theologians are accustomed to saying that the cause of the world's sickness is sin. Let us just say that the cause is human nature, with its tendency to live selfishly. Whittier, a Quaker mystic, put it thus:

> So to the calmly gathered thought
> The innermost of truth is taught,
> The mystery dimly understood,
> That love of God is love of good,
> And, chiefly, its divinest trace
> In him of Nazareth's holy face;
> That to be saved is only this,—
> Salvation from our selfishness. . . .

The Taoist mystic stated that the time to deal with problems is before they grow too big. Now if the world's sickness is sin, a radical treatment of each individual is called for. True, we cannot avoid the necessity of dealing with big troubles, like wars and poverty. But it will be easier to deal with the smaller, more fundamental troubles by showing each person how much happier he will be when freed from self-centeredness.

The witness of all religions is the same: selfishness is the cause of most of the world's strife.

GOD HELP OUR NATION to live unselfishly in today's world, and help us to set an example of individual unselfishness. May we have sufficient wisdom to solve our big problems and greater wisdom to solve small problems before they grow big. Amen.

184 PATH OF WISDOM

OLD TESTAMENT

A soft answer turns away wrath,
  but a harsh word stirs up anger.

.   .   .   .

The lips of the wise spread knowledge;
  not so the minds of fools.

.   .   .   .

Better is a little with the fear of the Lord
  than great treasure and trouble with it.
Better is a dinner of herbs where love is
  than a fatted ox and hatred with it.

.   .   .   .

He who ignores instruction despises himself,
  but he who heeds admonition gains understanding.

.   .   .   .

Pride goes before destruction,
  and a haughty spirit before a fall.

.   .   .   .

He who is slow to anger is better than the mighty,
  and he who rules his spirit than he who takes a city.

.   .   .   .

If a man returns evil for good,
evil will not depart from his house.

PROVERBS 15:1, 7, 16-17, 32; 16:18, 32; 17:13

There is much unused wisdom in the Old Testament Proverbs. They are so true that we take them for granted—and then forget to use them. But by prayerful meditation, we may cultivate the kindly manner, friendly communication, contentment, humility, power of personality, and the generosity of greatness—virtues all beautifully presented in the memorable passages quoted above.

If any of us lack wisdom, it is certainly not for want of it in the world's great scriptures.

GOD MAKE US ever responsive to words of wisdom that lead to peace and happiness within and without. May wisdom and love be our only masters. Amen.

185 PROGRESSING TOGETHER

ZOROASTRIANISM

May we be those who shall make life progressive or purposeful!
Assemble together, along with Justice, O Ahuras Mazda, and come
*   hither*
So that there where our thoughts formerly developed separately,
*   they may now mature together, fuse, and become wisdom.*

.   .   .   .

Since the preferable path is not always obvious
Therefore, as heaven appointed arbiter and judge over both
*   parties,*
Will I go to you, that we may live in accordance with Justice.

YASNA 30-31

The individual can do little without the co-operation of his fellows. The most effective thing he can do is to initiate some enterprise that may lead to common wisdom and happiness. Zoroaster understood this, for in the above passage he urged progress through "togetherness." Wisdom begins with individuals, but needs the co-operation of the community for its perfection and implementation. "The preferable path is not always obvious." When separate thoughts fuse and mature together, a very practical type of wisdom emerges. The thoughts of one stimulate the thinking of another. This is democratic procedure; it is infinitely better than unilateral rule anywhere.

The great prophets agree that democratic procedure is applicable everywhere, since all of God's children are capable of maturing in wisdom.

GOD HELP US to give others due credit for their share of the wisdom of experience, as together we attack common problems for common purposes. May we be wise enough to seek this partnership of wisdom within the will of God. Amen.

186 REFLECTING GLORY

HINDUISM

The sunlight is one and the same wherever it falls, but only bright surfaces like water, mirrors and polished metals can reflect it fully. So is the divine light. It falls equally and impartially on all hearts, but only the pure and clean hearts of the good and holy can fully reflect it. RAMAKRISHNA

If all are children of God, it is because the sunlight of God's wisdom and love falls equally upon all of us. Unfortunately not all of us reflect that wisdom and love equally. Why not? According to Ramakrishna, whose sayings are revered by many, it is because not all hearts are equally pure and clean and good and holy. Perhaps he has hit upon the most important part of the explanation. But there are also differences of intelligence among us; some people are more limited than others by the degree of their capacity to learn and understand. Yet even these, by keeping their hearts pure and good, can reflect the glory of God and bring to shame others who have more intelligence. After all, God asks no more than that we use the talents that we have.

Pure hearts are wise hearts; clean hearts are kind.

> O God,
>> Our hearts are thine;
>> So let them shine
>>> Reflecting thy pure glory.   Amen.

187   DELIGHT IN THE LAW

OLD TESTAMENT

> *Blessed is the man*
>> *who walks not in the counsel of the wicked,*
> *nor stands in the way of sinners,*
>> *nor sits in the seat of the scoffers;*
> *but his delight is in the law of the Lord,*
>> *and on his law he meditates day and night.*
> *He is like a tree*
>> *planted by streams of water,*
> *that yields its fruit in its season,*
>> *and its leaf does not wither.*
> *In all that he does, he prospers.*

The wicked are not so,
  but are like chaff which the wind drives away.
Therefore the wicked will not stand in the judgment,
  nor sinners in the congregation of the righteous;
for the Lord knows the way of the righteous,
  but the way of the wicked will perish.

PSALM 1

This beautiful scripture asserts that the happy man is the good and sincere man, who loves to meditate on divine ways and prospers as the wicked do not. Now we know that many a good man does not prosper and that he has little to make him happy. Nevertheless, the Psalm is essentially true if by "prosper" we mean that his good deeds lead to the enjoyment of God's companionship and to fellowship with all men of good will. What other kind of prosperity and happiness do we want? This is a Psalm worth memorizing and repeating to ourselves in times of adversity, for consolation and spiritual strength.

After all, if wickedness is antisocial attitude and inward conflict, how can it lead to happiness or to ultimate salvation?

GRACIOUS GOD, give us grace to believe in the blissfulness of goodness and in the prosperity of contentment. Amen.

188 SPRINGS IN THE DESERT

OLD TESTAMENT

Say to those who are of a fearful heart,
  "Be strong, fear not!
Behold, your God
  will come . . . and save you."

205

Then the eyes of the blind shall be opened,
  and the ears of the deaf unstopped. . . .
For waters shall break forth in the wilderness,
  and streams in the desert. . . .

And a highway shall be there,
  and it shall be called the Holy Way . . .
  the redeemed shall walk there.
And the ransomed of the Lord shall return . . .
  with everlasting joy . . .
  and sorrow and sighing shall flee away.

ISAIAH 35:4-10 passim

The resources of the universe are ample and available to those who seek confidence in man's salvation. There is much to be done by way of opening the eyes of those whose spiritual sight is poor, who thirst for wisdom and love, and who walk with tragedy. One of the values of foreign travel is that it opens the eyes of many who had thought themselves to be poor, so that they now realize how desperate much of the world is. The poverty of the world is twofold: material and spiritual. But God is great, and his spirit can work in us to cause springs to break forth in the wilderness.

Perhaps as our world grows smaller and more closely knit, some of us will not let the rest of us suffer in soul and body.

GOD MAKE US humble and committed to a life of service, designed to channel the rich resources of the universe to the spiritual and material needs of men. Amen.

THAT YOUR SOUL MAY LIVE

Ho, every one who thirsts,
come to the waters,
and he who has no money,
come, buy and eat!
Come, buy wine and milk
without money and without price.
Why do you spend your money for that which is not bread,
and your labor for that which does not satisfy?
Hearken diligently to me, and eat what is good,
and delight yourselves in fatness.
Incline your ear, and come to me;
hear, that your soul may live;
and I will make with you an everlasting covenant. . . .

ISAIAH 55:1-3

He who sees deeply will realize that the most essential need of man is spiritual. With the vision of love and the enlightenment of knowledge and wisdom, men of the world will be enabled to do for themselves those things for which they now experience such desperate need. Meanwhile in our Western material culture we tend to put our trust in bombs and other things which money can buy. We cannot do much toward the spiritual enlightenment of mankind as long as this is the case. Genuine fellowship between men of good will, with virtuous living, is a prerequisite to world peace and prosperity.

Need we have doubt concerning the abundance of spiritual food for everybody everywhere, when we think of the prophets whom God has sent into all cultures?

GRACIOUS GOD,
> Open my eyes, that I may see
> Glimpses of truth thou hast for me;
> Place in my hands the wonderful key
> That shall unclasp, and set me free. Amen.

190 DEDICATED LEADERSHIP

CONFUCIANISM

Do not let him oppress the friendless and childless, nor let him fear the high and distinguished. When men in office have ability and administrative power, let them be made still more to cultivate their conduct; and the prosperity of the country will be promoted. All such right men, having a competency, will go on in goodness.   SHU CHING 5.4.3.5

A great Confucian scholar thus summarizes Confucius' views on government and education:

> The proper aim of government is the welfare and happiness of the whole people.
>
> This aim can be achieved only when the state is administered by those most capable of government.
>
> Capacity to govern has no necessary connection with birth, wealth, or position; it depends solely on character and knowledge.
>
> Character and knowledge are produced by proper education.
>
> In order that the best talents may become available, education should be widely diffused.
>
> It follows that the government should be administered by those persons, chosen from the whole population, who prove themselves to have profited most by the proper kind of education.

In a democracy, besides preparing ourselves for service we could all exercise greater care in selecting dedicated people to represent us in public office and in private organizations.

O GOD, whatever our task, may we be dedicated to impartial service. Help us to regard our civic duties as a sacred trust. Amen.

191 UNINNOCENT DESTRUCTION

JUDAISM

(Slander) slays three persons: the speaker, the spoken to, and the spoken of. . . . Whoever speaks slander is as though he denied the fundamental principle (i.e. the existence of God); whoever speaks slander is deserving of being stoned to death; the Holy One, blessed be he, says of such a person, I and he cannot dwell together in the world; whoever speaks slander magnifies iniquities equal to the three sins of idolatry, unchastity, and bloodshed. . . . The retailer of slander, the receiver of it, and who gives false evidence against his fellow, deserve to be cast to the dogs. . . . Let the honor of your neighbor be as dear to you as your own. . . . Just as a man esteems his own honor, so let him esteem the honor of his neighbor. Just as nobody wishes his own reputation slandered, so let him never desire to slander his neighbor's reputation. TALMUD

It is surprising how many people, otherwise good, will use their tongues to do irreparable injury to their neighbors through slander. It is hard to justify under any circumstances the repetition of vilifying reports about our associates. Such reports are more likely than not to turn out to be much worse than the real facts, since it is human nature

to want to tell a strange story. Was the Talmud unduly
harsh in its judgment of slander? Yet it is true that careless
reports often do more damage than physical wounds. Perhaps we should be like the woman who insisted on saying
something good about everyone, even remarking of the
devil, "Well, he is very industrious."

In most circumstances, unless some good purpose is to
be served by telling the evil report, it might truly be best
to bridle the tongue.

O God, may conscience keep us from slander at all times
and restrain our speech to kindly purposes. Give us the
courage to curb our careless tongues. Amen.

192 THE GOOD WILL

CONFUCIANISM

*Benevolence is the tranquil habitation of man, and righteous-
ness is his straight path.*
*Alas for them, who leave the tranquil dwelling empty, and do
not reside in it, and who abandon the right path and do not pursue it!*   MENCIUS 4
*Of the adage, "Only a good man knows how to like people,
knows how to dislike them," the Master said, He whose heart is
in the smallest degree set upon goodness will dislike no one.*

ANALECTS 4.3-4

The benevolent attitude toward all men is something that
needs to be cultivated, like a garden. If left alone, it tends
to be lost among the weeds. Prophets and other great men
are remembered for the persistent manner in which they
cultivated kindness, love, and the habit of service. Lincoln's

Second Inaugural Address well expresses his constant benevolence: "With malice toward none; with charity for all; with firmness in the right, as God gives us to see the right, let us strive on to finish the work we are in; to bind up the nation's wounds; to care for him who shall have borne the battle, and for his widow, and his orphan—to do all which may achieve and cherish a just and lasting peace among ourselves, and with all nations."

The house of hate is much less happy than the house of benevolence, both inwardly and in outward influence.

O GOD, may our good will be more than a pleasant sentiment. May we love with the strength of sincerity and the power of daily practice. Amen.

193 YOU SHALL BE HOLY

OLD TESTAMENT

And the Lord said to Moses, "Say to all the congregation of the people of Israel, You shall be holy; for I the Lord your God am holy. Every one of you shall revere his mother and his father, and you shall keep my sabbaths: I am the Lord your God. Do not turn to idols or make for yourselves molten gods: I am the Lord your God. . . . You shall not steal, nor deal falsely, nor lie to one another. And you shall not swear by my name falsely, and so profane the name of your God: I am the Lord. . . . You shall do no injustice in judgment; you shall not be partial to the poor or defer to the great, but in righteousness shall you judge your neighbor. . . . You shall not hate your brother in your heart, but you shall reason with your neighbor, lest you bear sin because of him. You shall not take vengeance or bear any grudge against the sons of your own people, but you shall love your

*neighbor as yourself: I am the Lord. . . . The stranger who
sojourns with you shall be to you as the native among you, and
you shall love him as yourself; for you were strangers in the land
of Egypt. . . .*   EXODUS 19:1-4, 11-12, 15, 17-18, 34

The word "holy" may suggest some mysterious quality.
But if we study its meaning in context, it seems to be
equivalent to the saying in Matthew, "Be perfect as your
heavenly Father is perfect." In the Exodus context, holiness
means filial respect, common morality, just living, and
benevolence to neighbors and strangers. In Matthew it
means the qualities of the sermon on the mount: humility,
mercy, purity of heart, peacemaking, kindly motivation,
and love toward all.

Since God is absolute perfection, we as God's children
can be satisfied with nothing less ourselves.

HEAVENLY FATHER, may we be grateful for the examples
of holy living set by those whom we revere. Amen.

194 SONS OF GOD

NEW TESTAMENT

*You have heard that it was said, "An eye for an eye and a
tooth for a tooth." But I say to you, Do not resist one who is
evil. But if any one strikes you on the right cheek, turn to him
the other also; and if any one would sue you and take your coat,
let him have your cloak as well; and if any one forces you to go
one mile, go with him two miles. Give to him who begs from you,
and do not refuse him who would borrow from you.*

*You have heard that it was said, "You shall love your neighbor
and hate your enemy." But I say to you, Love your enemies and
pray for those who persecute you, so that you may be sons of*

your Father who is in heaven; for he makes his sun rise on the evil and on the good, and sends rain on the just and on the unjust. For if you love those who love you, what reward have you? Do not even the tax collectors do the same? MATTHEW 5:38-46

We should be truly grateful for the courage of such ideals as are here expressed. It is the attitude of spirit that Jesus is aiming at, not a literal specification of conduct. Be generous to others, he is saying. Never close the door to the possibility that you may win your enemy to friendship. Nothing is to be gained by "getting even" with him since in that case he will still be your enemy. Take on the qualities of God's perfection, whose sun shines on the good and evil alike. God desires not revenge but moral and spiritual growth. Living by such divine ideals should be an exhilarating experience, far transcending any satisfaction from revenge and reciprocity.

How fascinating to live as children of God!

O GOD, give us the sense of our divine kinship and of thy power, that as thy children we may live generously and creatively. Amen.

195 THE DAY OF JUDGMENT

ZOROASTRIANISM

(In the Judgment Day) all men stand up; whoever is righteous and whoever is wicked, every human creature, they rouse up from the spot where its life departs. . . .

Then is the assembly of the Sadvastaran, where all mankind will stand at this time; in that assembly every one sees his own good deeds and his own evil deeds; and then, in that assembly, a wicked man becomes as conspiciuous as a white sheep. among those that are black. BUNDAHIS 30.7-10

The Zoroastrian concept of a resurrection and judgment has been most influential. The essential idea of judgment is true to human experience, whether in the present or in the dim future. Sam Walter Foss has expressed this fact:

And where is hell? And where is heaven? In some vague
    distance dim?
No, they are here and now in you—in me, in her, in him.
When is the Judgment Day to dawn? Its true date who can
    say?
Look in your calendar and see what day it is today!
Today is always Judgment Day; and Conscience throned
    within
Brings up before its judgment seat each soul to face his sin.
We march to judgment, each along an uncompanioned
    way—
Stand up, man, and accuse yourself and meet your Judg-
    ment Day.

Perhaps the fear of judgment can be lessened if we realize that our worse selves are constantly being judged by our better selves—as they should be.

GOD GIVE US good judgment as we live from day to day. May we approach the ideals of divine judgment as we direct our own principles of living. Amen.

I hate, I despise your feasts,
and I take no delight in your solemn assemblies. . . .
Take away from me the noise of your songs;
to the melody of your harps I will not listen.
But let justice roll down like waters,
and righteousness like an everflowing stream.

AMOS 5:21, 23-24

He has showed you, O man, what is good;
and what does the Lord require of you
but to do justice, and to love kindness,
and to walk humbly with your God?

MICAH 6:8

cease to do evil,
learn to do good;
seek justice,
correct oppression;
defend the fatherless,
plead for the widow.

ISAIAH 1:16-17

These verses represent a great tradition which has never been transcended. The insights are universal; their requirements are no less than the standards of perfection. The disgust of the skeptic concerning religious ritualism and hypocrisy is no more vehement than that of the great prophets. Pure religion is practical religion (James 1:27). The harm of ritual arises only when it becomes a substitute for practice. As symbols to fire the imagination and lead to action, religious forms may have much value. But the stress must always be on the experience of the heart.

Prophetic insight into today's practice of religion and ethics reveals much to criticize. We dare not be smug.

GOD MAKE US SINCERE; give us courage to rebel against meaningless ritual while we choose the substance of prophetic truth. Amen.

197 EXAMPLE OF SERVICE

NEW TESTAMENT

Jesus . . . rose from supper, laid aside his garments, and girded himself with a towel. Then he poured water into a basin, and began to wash the disciples' feet, and to wipe them with a towel with which he was girded.

. . . .

When he had washed their feet and taken his garments, and resumed his place, he said to them, "Do you know what I have done to you? You call me Teacher and Lord; and you are right, for so I am. If I then, your Lord and Teacher, have washed your feet, you also ought to wash one another's feet. For I have given you an example, that you also should do as I have done to you. Truly, truly, I say to you, a servant is not greater than his master; nor is he who is sent greater than he who sent him.

JOHN 13:3-5, 12-16

The dramatic character of the gospel story has strengthened its appeal throughout history. If our Lord and Teacher stooped to do a menial service, then we should never feel too dignified to do likewise. One thing we have learned from his example and our own experience is that real and lasting happiness comes through the practice of serving our fellow man, bringing what happiness we can to others. If we were

216

to make a list of the most happy people, we would begin not with dilettantes and playboys but with people like St. Francis of Assisi and Albert Schweitzer—servants of God and man, motivated by true insight into the divine character of human worth. Writes Radhakrishnan, a dedicated teacher and statesman of India, "Each individual is infinitely precious in God's eyes, whatever be his rank or position in society. By contemplation we develop a deep sense of piety towards life. We can improve the social order only when we wholeheartedly strive for justice and equality for all and accept individual responsibility for achieving this end."

Such words express a Christian conviction shared by the great of all faiths.

O GOD, may the story of Jesus' love and service be more than a sentimental memory. May we daily discern the Master near us as he longs for a comforting word or the gift of ourselves. Amen.

198   FRET NOT

OLD TESTAMENT

Be still before the Lord, and wait patiently for him;
  fret not yourself over him who prospers in his way,
  over the man who carries out evil devices!

Refrain from anger, and forsake wrath!
  Fret not yourself; it tends only to evil.
For the wicked shall be cut off;
  but those who wait for the Lord shall possess the land.
Yet a little while, and the wicked will be no more;

though you look well at his place, he will not be there.
But the meek shall possess the land,
  and delight themselves in abundant prosperity.

.   .   .   .

Better is a little that the righteous has
  than the abundance of many wicked.

PSALM 37:7-11, 16

Some men despair of ever finding happiness. Others miss happiness by aiming too directly at it in their fundamental concern for themselves. All desire it—or what we might call peace of mind. The commonest cause of missing such joy is worry. People worry about many things. They complain about what they do not have; about being surpassed by the Joneses; about their physical condition of cold or heat, or limitations of health or strength; about their income, or their unbeautiful features. Some complain about their moral weakness or intellectual failures. Others, like the Psalmist's friend, fret over the injustice of the universe. Now we need to be concerned about the realization of values, but not to the extent of worry.

To care about anything is to show an earnest desire to improve it. To worry and fret is to display a lack of faith.

O GOD, give us confidence in thy goodness and power. May we find the opportunities for service so absorbing that we never worry or complain about ourselves. Amen.

He is my Self within the heart, smaller than a corn of rice, smaller than a corn of barley, smaller than a mustard-seed, smaller than a canary seed or the kernel of a canary seed. He is my Self within the heart, greater than the earth, greater than the sky, greater than the heaven, greater than all these worlds.
CHANDOGYA UPANISHAD 3.14.3

He who is self-created is Bliss. A man experiences happiness by tasting that Bliss. Who could breathe, who could live, if that Bliss did not exist in his heart?   TAITTIRIYA UPANISHAD 2.7.1

They say lightning is Brahman.
BRIHADARANYAKA UPANISHAD 5.7.1

It is like a flash of lightning; it is like a wink of the eye.
KENA UPANISHAD 4.4

His form is not an object of vision; no one beholds him with the eye.   KATHA UPANISHAD 2.3.9

In the beginning, my dear, there was That only which is one only, without a second.   CHANDOGYA UPANISHAD 6.2.1

Perhaps the deepest cause of unhappiness is the fundamental failure to accept existence with all that it entails. The virtue of Hinduism is its complete acceptance of the world as the living manifestation of God. In any tradition whatsoever, it is the mystic who abandons himself to the mercies of God in his universe with thrilling ecstasy, as did Rabindranath Tagore, the Hindu poet:

I know now God offers affection in the form of a mother,
in the form of a son He accepts it again.
In the form of a donor He gives,
he takes again in the form of the poor.

As a disciple He shows his devotion,
as a teacher He gives his blessings.
As a beloved breaking the stony heart
he raises in it the fountain of love.
He is all attached; he is also the renouncer.
In this God's teeming universe,
I have cast the net of my heart:
the entire world is drawing me, pulling me
into the lap of its love.
This great bond has filled my heart
with its joy and its sorrow.

One thing seems certain—that the greatest happiness is
hidden from those who have no faith or experience of God.

O GOD, we would know thee face to face, with a knowledge that is by faith yet firmly assured through the evidence of our most persistent intuitions. Amen.

200 ONE FOLD

NEW TESTAMENT

*Welcome one another, therefore, as Christ has welcomed you,
for the glory of God. For I tell you that Christ became a servant
to the circumcised to show God's truthfulness, in order to con-
firm the promises given to the patriarchs, and in order that the
Gentiles might glorify God for his mercy. As it is written,*

> *"Therefore I will praise thee among the Gentiles,
>   and sing to thy name";*

and again it is said,

220

> *"Rejoice, O Gentiles, with his people";*

and again,

> *"Praise the Lord, all Gentiles,*
> *and let all the peoples praise him";*

and further Isaiah says,

> *"The root of Jesse shall come,*
> *he who rises to rule the Gentiles;*
> *in him shall the Gentiles hope."*

May the God of hope fill you with all joy and peace in believing,
so that by the power of the Holy Spirit you may abound in hope.
ROMANS 15:7-13

In the preceding chapter Paul had said, "As for the man who is weak in faith, welcome him, but not for disputes over opinions. One believes he may eat anything, while the weak man eats only vegetables. Let not him who eats despise him who abstains, and let not him who abstains pass judgment on him who eats; for God has welcomed him. Who are you to pass judgment on the servant of another? It is before his own master that he stands or falls. And he will be upheld, for the Master is able to make him stand.

"One man esteems one day as better than another, while another man esteems all days alike. Let every one be fully convinced in his own mind" (Romans 14:1-5).

There is much in the Christian tradition to justify the attitude of sincere sympathy and fellowship with those of all faiths, as expressed in their great scriptures. Jesus himself said, "And I have other sheep, that are not of this fold; I must bring them also, and they will heed my voice. So there shall be one flock, one shepherd" (John 10:16).

The Apostle Paul had not the advantage of knowing the

great scriptures of the world. No doubt he would still commend his Master as the pre-eminent hope of the world in its present distress.

The Lord bless you and keep you:
The Lord make his face to shine upon you, and be gracious
    to you:
The Lord lift up his countenance upon you, and give you
    peace. NUMBERS 6:24-26

NOTES ON SOURCES

The list of sources below is designed to supplement the references given in the meditations themselves. More detailed bibliographical information may be found in the Acknowledgments and Bibliography of Sources, beginning on page 229, or on the copyright page.

Where no line number is indicated, a source listed below refers to the scripture passage which appears in *italic* type at the opening of each meditation. Line numbers are given only for sources of quotations to be found within the author's commentary, which follows the opening scripture passage and appears in roman type in every meditation; numbering begins with the first line of roman type in each meditation.

Meditation
Number

1   All Biblical quotations are from *The Holy Bible,* Revised Standard Version, copyrighted 1946, 1952 by the Division of Christian Education of the National Council of Churches of Christ in the U. S. A.

2   Tr. Guthrie. All subsequent passages from the Gathas (Yasnas) are Guthrie's.

3   Breasted, *Dawn of Conscience,* p. 282.

4   Tr. Griffith. All subsequent passages from the Rig-Veda are Griffith's.

6   Koran 6:12, 59 is quoted from Ameer Ali, *Spirit of Islam,* p. 145. The reference to 6:12 seems in error. But see 6:2-3, 104; 50: 15; 67:12-14. Koran 2:109 is Rodwell's translation. All subsequent passages from the Koran are Rodwell's unless otherwise noted.

7   Lines 3-4: *Confessions* 1.1.1.

10 Tr. Müller, in *Sacred Books of the East* (hereafter referred to as *SBE*).

11 Tr. Hume.

12 Tr. Hume.

13 Tr. Nikhilananda.

14 Tr. Nikhilananda.

15 Tr. Müller, *SBE.*
    Lines 7-12: Lucien Price, *Dialogues of Alfred North Whitehead,* final paragraph.

16 Archer, *Sikhs,* pp. 53-54.

18 Tr. Blakney. All quotations from the Tao Tê Ching are from R. B. Blakney's translation unless otherwise noted. The Chuang Tzu quotation, lines 10-11, is also from Blakney, *Way of Life,* p. 4.

Meditation
Number

20   Lines 8-16: Ameer Ali, *Spirit of Islam*, p. 150.
21   Lines 7-10: Kierkegaard, *Purity of Heart*, p. 206.
      Lines 12-13: *Ibid.*, p. 217.
      Lines 18-23: *Ibid.*, p. 218.
22   Lines 19-20: Matthew 5:48.
23   Lines 15-17: Charles Wesley, *Divine Love.*
24   Macauliffe, *Sikh Religion* 6, pp. 105 f., quoted in Jack Finegan,
      Archeology of World Religions, p. 545.
25   Mrs. Rhys Davids, *SBE.*
26   Anesaki, *Japanese Religion*, p. 133.
27   Tr. Nikhilananda.
      Lines 10-13: Croly, *Spirit of God*, quoted from *The Methodist
      Hymnal.*
28   Lines 11-14: "Aurora Leigh."
29   Lines 7-20: *Bibliolatres.*
30   Lines 4-8: Mei Yi-Pao, *Works of Motse*, chap. 27.
      Lines 9-13: Luke 6:35-36.
35   Cohen, *Everyman's Talmud*, p. 119.
36   Lines 11-15: Spinoza, *Ethics*, Part 1, Appendix.
      Lines 15-17: Mencius 7, tr. Wong. All passages from Mencius,
      The Great Learning, and *The Doctrine of the Mean*, cited
      hereafter, are by Wong unless otherwise noted. See Ballou,
      Bible of the World, p. 1358.
38   Lines 4-15: Tennyson, "In Memoriam."
40   Lines 14-15: Stevenson, *Child's Garden of Verses.*
41   Prabhavananda and Isherwood. All subsequent quotations are
      from their translation unless otherwise noted.
42   Tr. Bhagwat.
      Lines 5-6: Shih Ching, Legge, *Chinese Classics*, vol. 4, pt. 2.
44   Westminster Shorter Catechism 10.
45   Tr. Bhagwat.
47   Bhagavad-Gita 2, with comment, from Gandhi, *Autobiography*,
      p. 90.
49   Tr. Wilson.
50   Cohen, *Everyman's Talmud*, p. 87.
52   Tr. Waley, in *Three Ways of Thought*, pp. 21-22.
53   Waley. All subsequent quotations from the *Analects* are by
      Waley unless otherwise noted.
      Lines 9-16: Whittier, "The Eternal Goodness."
54   Lines 1-4: Carlyle, *Heroes and Hero Worship*, Lecture 1.
      Lines 5-6, 10-11: For Luther, see also Bainton, *Here I Stand*,
      pp. 179, 185.
      Lines 11-12: Talmud, tr. Polano, 1876, p. 310. Runes ed., p. 92.
55   Lines 13-23: Whittier, "The Over-Heart."

56 Tr. Radhakrishnan. All subsequent passages from the Dhamma-
    pada are by Radhakrishnan unless otherwise noted.
57 Lines 9-20: Tennyson, "In Memoriam."
58 *The Apocrypha,* Revised Standard Version.
59 Tr. Rhys Davids, *SBE.*
60 Tr. Chalmers.
61 Conze, *Buddhist Texts,* p. 131.
62 Tr. Jacobi, *SBE.*
63 Archer, *Sikhs,* pp. 125-26.
64 Lines 13-18: Thomas Curtis Clarke, "The Search."
65 Tr. from the Greek by Q. M. Lyon.
67 Lines 8-13: Emerson, *Woodnotes.*
68 Anesaki, *Religious Life,* pp. 28-29.
    Lines 18-21: Tennyson, "Locksley Hall."
69 Tr. Nikhilananda.
70 Tr. Hume.
71 Hume's translation, except 3.17.1, which is Müller's, *SBE.*
72 Avalon, *Shakti,* pp. 29-30.
75 *Analects* 6.16, tr. Ware.
    Lines 1-2: This and all subsequent quotations from Rama-
      krishna are from Abhedananda, *The Sayings of Ramakrishna.*
    Lines 5-10: Li Chi, Legge, *SBE.*
76 Tr. Bhagwat.
79 Lines 7-11: Mencius 7.
    Lines 12-13: Shu Ching 4.2.4, Legge, *SBE.* All subsequent quota-
      tions from the Shu Ching are by Legge, *SBE.*
    Lines 14-16: Mencius 7.
    Line 16: Talmud 1876, p. 307. Runes ed., p. 89.
    Lines 17-19: James 2:18.
80 "The Forty-Two Traditions of An-Nawawi" 26, tr. Bishop.
    Lines 13-16: Matthew 23:23.
81 Lines 7-23: Radhakrishnan, *Religion and Society,* p. 98.
82 Legge, *Chinese Classics,* vol. 4, pt. 2.
    Lines 13-27: Kierkegaard, *The Lilies of the Field,* p. 219.
83 Lines 5-11: *Ibid.,* pp. 210, 211.
84 Tr. Creel, in *Chinese Thought,* pp. 128-29. Professor Creel refers
      to Duyvendak, "Hsuntzu on the Rectification of Names."
    Lines 2-6: *Analects* 7.16, tr. Ware.
85 Lines 13-23: Oxenham, "Some Blesseds."
87 Lines 11-17: *Ibid.*
91 Tr. Bhagwat.
94 Lines 1-5: Bradley, "My Station and Its Duties," in *Ethical
    Studies.*

95   Lines 9-12: Plato, *The Republic,* 1.335, Jowett.
96   Mei, *Works of Mo-Tzŭ,* chap. 46.
     Lines 7-19: *Ibid.,* chap. 15.
97   *Tao Tê Ching* 79, tr. Ch'u Ta-Kao.
101   Mei, Works of Mo-Tzŭ, chap. 16.
103   Talmud 1876, p. 260. Runes ed., p. 44.
105   Li Chi, Legge, *SBE.*
106   Hsiao Ching (Book of Filial Duty) 5, tr. Ivan Chen.
111   Talmud 1876, p. 241. Runes ed., p. 26.
     Lines 4-6: Mahabharata 5.1517, quoted from Browne, *World's Great Scriptures,* Preface.
     Lines 7-8: *Analects* 15.23, Legge, *SBE.*
     Lines 9-11: *Analects* 6.23, Legge, *SBE.*
     Lines 12-14: "The Forty-Two Traditions of An-Nawawi" 13, tr. Bishop.
     Lines 14-15: Udana-Varga 5.18, quoted from Browne, *idem.*
113   Lines 2-3: Emporia *Gazette,* Nov. 17, 1923.
     Lines 3-5: Emerson, "Self-Reliance."
114   Peet, *Proverbs of Ptahhotep,* p. 101.
117   *Tao Tê Ching* 8, Giles.
118   *Tao Tê Ching* 78, Giles.
     Lines 4-7: Isaiah 40:31.
     Lines 13-16: T. S. Eliot, "Ash Wednesday," 6. *Complete Poems and Plays,* p. 67.
     Lines 17-19: T. S. Eliot, "Shakespeare and the Stoicism of Seneca." *Selected Essays 1917-1932,* p. 111.
119   Lines 1-2: Edmund Burke, "Second Speech on Conciliation," The Thirteen Resolutions.
120   "The Forty-Two Traditions of An-Nawawi" 32, tr. Bishop.
     Lines 11-12: Rousseau, *Emile,* Book 2.
122   Lines 15-16: Thoreau, "Civil Disobedience."
124   Tr. Bhagwat.
125   Line 3: La Rochefoucauld, Maxim 218.
127   Tr. Budge, pp. 366-71.
128   Tr. Thomas, *Life of Buddha,* pp. 87-88.
130   Tr. Thomas.
131   Tr. Thomas.
134   Lines 3-4: *Analects* 14:29.
     Lines 4-5: Matthew 7:16.
138   Mencius, Legge, Chinese Classics, pt. 1.
139   *Dhammapada* 165, Bhagwat.
140   Lines 1-8: Radhakrishnan, *The Dhammapada,* p. 101.
142   Mencius, Legge, *Chinese Classics,* pt. 1.

143 Soko's lecture notes on Bushido (17th century), in Anesaki, *Japanese Religion*, pp. 279-80.

145 King, *Letters and Inscriptions of Hammurapi.*

147 Fung, *Short History of Chinese Philosophy*, p. 63.
Lines 6-7: For Edward Everett Hale, see Meditation 122.
Lines 12-15: Fung, *Ibid.*, p. 61.

149 Lines 15-22: Lowell, "The Present Crisis."

150 Lines 8-11: Markham, "Outwitted."

151 Kurosumi Kyosho, "The Texts of Kurozumi Kyo," in D. C. Holtom, *The National Faith of Japan*, p. 252.

153 Vasalasutta 21, Fausböll, *SBE* (=Uragavagga 135).

155 Legge.
Lines 17-20: Samuel Longfellow, "Holy Spirit, Truth Divine." *Methodist Hymnal.*

159 Konko Kyo Kyoten, "The Sacred Texts of Konko Kyo," in Holtom, *The National Faith of Japan*, pp. 261-62.

163 Koran 5:48, tr. by Ameer, *Spirit of Islam*, p. 175.

165 Archer, *The Sikhs*, p. 75.

166 Lines 7-8: Emerson, "Give All to Love."
Lines 10-12: Symonds, *Sonnet, On the Sacro Monte.*

169 Lines 15-20: Edwin Markham, "A Prayer."

170 Müller, *SBE.*

171 Jacobi, *SBE.*

172 Rhys Davids, *SBE.*

173 Shryock, *Origin and Development of the State Cult of Confucius*, p. 169.
Hsun-Tzu tr. by Creel, in *Chinese Thought*, p. 125. Professor Creel refers to Dubs, *Works of Hsuntze.*

174 West, *SBE.*

176 Lines 9-10: Tennyson, "Morte d'Arthur."
Lines 12-14: Tennyson, "In Memoriam."

177 Kurosumi Kyosho, "The Texts of Kurozumi Kyo," in Holtom, *The National Faith of Japan*, p. 252.
Lines 17-22: Matthew Arnold, "Desire."

178 Line 10: Tennyson, "Locksley Hall."
Lines 13-16: Santayana, *Poems*, p. 5.

180 Shih Ching, Legge, *Chinese Classics*, vol. 4, pt. 1.
Lines 11-12: Herrault de Sechelles, *Voyage à Montabar.*
Lines 12-13: Carlyle, "Frederick the Second," 4.3.

183 Lines 7-14: "The Meeting," lines 215-22.

189 Lines 16-19: Charles H. Scott, in *The Cokesbury Worship Hymnal*, no. 89.

190 Lines 3-17: Creel, *Confucius*, pp. 165-66.

191 Cohen, *Everyman's Talmud*, pp. 99-100.

Meditation
Number

193 Lines 3-4: Matthew 5:48.
195 West, *SBE*.
Lines 5-17: Sam Walter Foss, *The Higher Catechism*.
197 Lines 13-19: Radhakrishnan, *Recovery of Faith*, p. 167.
199 Tr. Nikhilananda.
Lines 8-22: *A Tagore Testament*, p. 21.

ACKNOWLEDGMENTS
AND
BIBLIOGRAPHY OF SOURCES

Grateful acknowledgment is hereby made to authors, publishers, and copyright owners for permission to quote from the books listed below. Additional credits are listed on the copyright page.

AMEER (THE RIGHT HON. SYED AMEER ALI). *The Spirit of Islam.* Rev. ed. New York: Harper & Brothers. London: Chatto and Windus, 1935.

ANESAKI, M. *History of Japanese Religion.* London: Routledge and Kegan Paul, 1930.

———. *Religious Life of the Japanese People.* Series on Japanese Life and Culture, vol. II. Tokyo: Society for International Cultural Relations, 1938.

Apocrypha, The. Revised Standard Version. New York: Thomas Nelson & Sons, 1957.

ARCHER, JOHN CLARK. *The Sikhs in Relation to Hindus, Moslems, Christians, and Ahmadiyyas.* Princeton: Princeton University Press, 1946.

AVALON (WOODROFFE, SIR JOHN G., *q.v.*).

BAINTON, ROLAND H. *Here I Stand.* Nashville: Abingdon Press, 1950.

Bhagavad-Gita: The Song of God. Tr. Swami Prabhavananda and Christopher Isherwood. Mentor Edition, New York: New American Library [Hollywood: Vedanta Society of Southern California], 1944.

BHAGWAT, N. K. *The Dhammapada.* Bombay: Dr. M. Venkatrao, J. P., President, The Buddha Society, Anand Vihara, Lamington Road, Bombay, 1955.

BIBLE: *The Holy Bible,* Revised Standard Version. New York: Thomas Nelson and Sons, 1946 and 1952.

Bible of the World. Ed. R. O. Ballou and F. Spiegelberg. New York: Viking Press, 1939.

BISHOP, ERIC F. F. (tr.). "The Forty-Two Traditions of An-Nawawi," *The Moslem World,* XXIX (April, 1939), 163-77. Published by the Hartford Seminary Foundation, Hartford, Conn. Also published in *The Bible of the World.*

BLAKNEY, R. B. *The Way of Life: Lao Tzu.* A new translation of the *Tao Tê Ching.* A Mentor Book. New York: New American Library of World Literature, 1955.

BRADLEY, FRANCIS H. *Ethical Studies.* New York: The Liberal Arts Press, 1951. First English edition, Oxford, 1876.

BREASTED, JAMES HENRY. *The Dawn of Conscience*. New York: Charles Scribner's Sons, 1947.

BROWNE, LEWIS. *The World's Great Scriptures*. New York: The Macmillan Company, 1946.

BUDDHA. *Further Dialogues of the Buddha*. Vol. I. Tr. Robert Chalmers, from the Majjhima Nikaya, for the Pali Text Society. London: Oxford University Press, 1926.

BUDGE, E. A. (tr.). *The Book of the Dead*. London: Routledge & Kegan Paul, 1953.

CARLYLE, THOMAS. *Heroes, Hero-Worship and the Heroic in History*. New York: The Macmillan Company, 1921.

CHEN, IVAN (tr.). *The Book of Filial Duty* (Hsiao Ching). Wisdom of the East Series. London: John Murray, 1920.

CH'U TA-KAO (tr.). *Tao Teh Ching*. London: The Buddhist Lodge, 1937.

CLARK, THOMAS CURTIS. *Love Off to the War and Other Poems*. James T. White and Company, 1918.

COHEN, A. (ed.). *Everyman's Talmud*. New York: E. P. Dutton and Company. London: J. M. Dent & Sons, Ltd., 1932.

The Cokesbury Worship Hymnal. Nashville: Cokesbury Press, 1938.

CONZE, EDWARD (ed.). *Buddhist Texts through the Ages*. New York: Philosophical Library, 1954.

CREEL, HERRLEE GLESSNER. *Chinese Thought: From Confucius to Mao Tse-tung*. Chicago: University of Chicago Press, 1953.

———. *Confucius: the Man and the Myth*. New York: John Day Company, 1949.

DAVIDS, MRS. RHYS, AND F. L. WOODWARD. *Kindred Sayings* (Samyutta), 3 vols. London: Oxford University Press, 1917, 1922, 1925.

ELIOT, T. S. *The Complete Poems and Plays*. New York: Harcourt, Brace and Company, 1952.

———. *Collected Poems 1909-1935*. London: Faber and Faber, Ltd.

———. *Selected Essays 1917-1932*. New York: Harcourt, Brace and Company. London: Faber and Faber, Ltd., 1932.

FINEGAN, JACK. *The Archeology of World Religions*. Princeton: Princeton University Press, 1952.

FOSS, SAM WALTER. *Dreams in Homespun*. Boston: Lothrop, Lee & Shepard Company, 1897.

FUNG, YU-LAN. *A Short History of Chinese Philosophy*. Ed. Derk Bodde. New York: The Macmillan Company, 1948.

GANDHI, MOHANDAS K. *Gandhi's Autobiography*. Washington: Public Affairs Press, 1954.

GILES, LIONEL. *Sayings of Lao Tzu*. Wisdom of the East Series. London: John Murray, 1905.

GRIFFITH, RALPH T. H. (tr.). *Hymns of the Rig-Veda*. 2 vols. Benares: E. J. Lazarus and Company, 1896.

Guthrie, Kenneth S. (tr.). *The Hymns of Zoroaster*. Brooklyn: Comparative Literature, 1914. London: George Bell, 1914.

Hill, Caroline Miles. *The World's Great Religious Poetry*. New York: The Macmillan Company, 1923.

Holtom, Daniel C. *The National Faith of Japan*. London: Kegan Paul, 1938.

"Hsun-tzu on the Rectification of Names," tr. J. J. L. Duyvendak, in *T'oung Pao* XXIII. Leiden: E. J. Brill, 1924.

Hsun Tzu. *The Works of Hsuntze, translated from the Chinese, with notes*, by Homer H. Dubs. Probsthain's Oriental Series. London: Probsthain, 1928.

Kierkegaard, Sören. *Edifying Discourses*. New York: Harper & Brothers, 1958.

———. *The Gospel of Suffering and The Lilies of the Field*. Minneapolis: Augsburg Publishing House, 1948.

———. *Purity of Heart*. New York: Harper & Brothers, 1948.

King, L. W. *The Letters and Inscriptions of Hammurapi*. London: Luzac, 1900.

Konko. *The Sacred Scriptures of Konkokyo*, with an introduction, translated and edited by Konkokyo hombu. Okayama-ken, Konkocho, 1933.

Koran, The. Tr. J. M. Rodwell. Second Revised and Amended Edition. London: Bernard Quaritch, 1876.

Legge, James. *Chinese Classics*, pt. 1. Boston: Houghton Mifflin Company, 1882. 4 vols. London: Trubner and Company, 1871.

Lyon, Quinter M. *The Great Religions*. New York: Odyssey Press, 1957.

Macauliffe, Max A. *The Sikh Religion, Its Gurus, Sacred Writings, and Authors*. 6 vols. Oxford: Clarendon Press, 1909.

Markham, Edwin. *The Man with the Hoe, and Other Poems*. New York: Doubleday, Page and Company, 1926.

———. *The Shoes of Happiness and Other Poems*. New York: Doubleday, Page and Company, 1915.

———. *Poems of Edwin Markham*. Ed. Charles L. Wallis. New York: Harper & Brothers, 1950.

Masnavi, The. Tr. C. E. Wilson. London: Probsthain, 1910.

Methodist Hymnal. Nashville: Methodist Publishing Company, 1939.

Morgan, Evan. *Tao, the Great Luminant*. Hong Kong: Kelly & Walsh, 1934.

Mo-Tzŭ. *The Ethical and Political Works of Motse*. Tr. Mei Yi-Pao. London: Probsthain, 1929.

Nikhilananda, Swami (ed. and tr.). *The Upanishads*. 3 vols. New York: Harper & Brothers, 1949, 1952, 1956.

Oxenham, John. *The Vision Splendid*. New York: George H. Doran Company, 1917.

Page, Curtis Hidden. *Chief American Poets*. New York: Houghton Mifflin Company, 1905.

PEET, T. ERIC. *A Comparative Study of the Literature of Egypt, Palestine, and Mesopotamia.* London: Oxford University Press, 1931.

Plato's Dialogues, 4 vols., tr. Jowett. 4th ed. Oxford: Clarendon Press, 1953.

PRZYWARA, ERICH (arr.). *An Augustine Synthesis.* New York: Harper & Brothers, 1958.

RADHAKRISHNAN, SARVEPALLI. *The Dhammapada.* London: Oxford University Press, 1950.

———. *The Recovery of Faith.* New York: Harper & Brothers, 1955.

———. *Religion and Society.* New York: The Macmillan Company. London: George Allen and Unwin, 1947.

RAMAKRISHNA. *The Sayings of Ramakrishna.* Abhedananda. New York: The Vedanta Society, 1903.

Sacred Books of the East. Ed. Max Müller. American Edition. 12 vols. New York: Charles Scribner's Sons, 1897-1901. Original English Edition. 50 vols. Oxford: Clarendon Press, 1897.

SANTAYANA, GEORGE. *Poems.* New York: Charles Scribner's Sons, 1923.

SHRYOCK, JOHN K. *The Origin and Development of the State Cult of Confucius.* New York. Century, 1932; copyright 1932 by the American Historical Association.

SPINOZA. *Works of Spinoza.* Tr. R. H. M. Elwes. London: George Bell and Son, 1887.

TAGORE. *A Tagore Testament.* Tr. Indu Dutt. New York: Philosophical Library, 1954.

Talmud. Selections. Tr. H. Polano. Philadelphia: Claxton, Remsen & Haffelfinger, 1876.

Talmud of Jerusalem, The. Ed. Dagobert D. Runes, tr. H. Polano. New York: Philosophical Library, 1956.

THOMAS, EDWARD J. *The Life of Buddha as Legend and History.* New York: Alfred A. Knopf. London: Routledge & Kegan Paul, 1927.

UPANISHADS: *The Thirteen Principal Upanishads.* Tr. Robert E. Hume. 2nd ed. London: Oxford University Press, 1931.

WALEY, ARTHUR. *The Analects of Confucius.* New York: The Macmillan Company. London: George Allen & Unwin, 1938. Reprinted 1945.

———. *Three Ways of Thought in Ancient China.* New York: The Macmillan Company. London: George Allen and Unwin, 1939.

WARE, JAMES R. *The Sayings of Confucius.* New York: New American Library, 1955.

WHITEHEAD. *Dialogues of Alfred North Whitehead,* as recorded by Lucien Price. Boston: Little, Brown & Company, 1954.

WONG, CHARLES A. *The Analects of Confucius. The Great Learning. The Doctrine of the Mean. The Works of Mencius.* No publisher. No date.

WOODROFFE, SIR JOHN G. *Shakti; or, The World as Power.* London: Women's Printing Society, 1920.

INDEX OF SCRIPTURES

(The numbers in parentheses refer to the meditation.)